A Christian FAMILY AC

Turn off the TV

Let's have fun instead!

Turn off the TV

Let's have fun instead!

KATHY BENCE

Collins

MARSHALL·PICKERING

First published in Great Britain
in 1990 by Marshall Pickering

Marshall Pickering is an imprint of
Collins Religious Division, part of
the Collins Publishing Group,
8 Grafton Street, London W1X 3LA

Copyright © 1990 Kathy Bence

Designed by Marion Morris

Text set in Palacio by
Avocet Robinson, Buckingham
Printed in Great Britain by
Richard Clay Ltd, Bungay, Suffolk

Contents

Acknowledgements

I want to thank my family upon whom so many experiments were tried, and also to thank all the families of the St Andrew's Baptist Church who have so inspired me.

Special thanks to our parents who lovingly made 'family' a commitment.

Also special thanks go to the Morgans, Willises, Mitchells and many other unnamed families who have blessed us by their example.

Introduction

"When we step into the family, by the act of being born, we do step into a world which is incalculable, into a world which has its own strange laws, into a world which could do without us, into a world that we have not made. In other words, WHEN WE STEP INTO THE FAMILY WE STEP INTO A FAIRY TALE."

(G.K. Chesterton)

These are days of uncertainty and fear. Under the pressures of modern life, God's ideal for the family can get lost in the shuffle. The above quotation from Chesterton makes us look at life afresh. *We are born into a fairy tale* – not, of course, in the sense that everyone automatically lives happily ever after (the end of the story belongs to God). But life in a family *is* an adventure, and it can be *magical*.

It is love which is the source of both adventure and of magic. We cannot choose the members of our family: we have to learn to love the ones who are there. I don't love Angela because she is perfect, but because she is my daughter. Learning to love those with whom we are placed (by God) is adventure enough for a lifetime. An adventure of learning – to accept others, to love God, to know myself.

And love is magic. Life does not give us all the money or time or talents we would have chosen, any more than it gives us the family we would have chosen. But I can decide to be happy with what I have, however much or little. I can create an oasis of love and acceptance in the midst of a desert. The very same people, the very same house and possessions that one person might want to complain about, can be transformed into a magical landscape by the love that accepts them unconditionally. The magic lies in changing one's point of view.

I write this book as a resource for families who accept the challenge of living life as an adventure. God has put us together for a purpose. We have to learn to love each other as he has loved us. But remember that the ideas in this book are only suggestions: you may want to try some but not others. The point is to stimulate your own creativity, and to give you things to try when the going gets hard. Treat the book as a buffet: take what you like and leave the rest. Sometimes you will try something and it will be a colossal failure. Never mind. As long as you can still laugh, even your failures will make great memories of family togetherness.

Loving is not easy. It forces us to deal with aspects of others that we do not like. It rubs us raw on the idiosyncrasies of others and their expectations of us. But all the while it is transforming us – and them. This is

God's plan for the world: stable family units, learning the reality of love at home, which they can then share with their neighbours and with the next generation.

Does this sound too idealistic? We may not be sure of living happily ever after, but we can try. And when God is part of the family, anything is possible!

Wesleyan Church Headquarters
Box 50434
Indianapolis, IN 46550-0434

Baptist Church Headquarters
Canal Street
Glasgow, Scotland

Rev. Eddie Shirras
Archdeacon of Northolt
71 Gayton Road
Harrow
Middlesex, HA1 2LY

Ms. Dale Hanson Bourke
c/o *Today's Christian Woman*
Gundusen Avenue
Carol Stream, Il

1 Making memories is an everyday event

You can make warm memories of everyday events by simply maximising on 'the moment'.

Bedtime with my 13-year-old daughter, Angela, is the time when she desires my closeness. Even at this 'mature' age, she likes me to climb under the covers with her and talk before she goes to sleep each night. Then it is that she tells me who she is and who she hopes to be.

Walks are ever so conducive to sharing deeply. Some of the best ever communication (with every member of my family) has taken place during a walk. Suggest a walk the next time you want to discuss something privately and successfully with a family member. Outings with individual children provide quality attention for maximum communication.

Angela likes nothing better than for the two of us to spend a day in Edinburgh shopping. We do not buy a lot, but we talk and talk, especially over lunch (usually pizza). This day spells 'L-O-V-E' to her, and she opens up her heart then as we relax together.

Whatever circumstances put your children in the mood to communicate, act on it before they are grown and the chance for memories is gone.

Weekends away with individual children

Individual children need individual attention – quality time alone with Mum or Dad. To meet this need, from about age eight or nine, plan a weekend away with each child each year. Alternate which parent goes with each child, to foster good communication with both parents.

As far as possible, allow your child to choose where you go and what you do. Budget may demand that you sleep at a relative's house, but *don't hang around there*. (I love to visit my relatives, but the goal of this trip is to be alone with my daughter. Explaining your goal to relatives should solve any misunderstanding.)

Then do whatever your child desires – not *your* pet hobby or sport. Concentrate on communicating with your child at his level. Find out his joys and fears, his dreams and likes. You may be surprised at how you can enjoy sausages and chips in your child's company.

No matter what you do, he will bask in this attention and blossom as a personality – because you've made him feel valuable and loved. You'll give him warm memories to keep him going through life's chillier moments. Best of all, you'll give him the impression that God is love, too.

Family portrait gallery

Some evening, drag out paper, paints, pen and ink or whatever medium the artists in your family like best.

Ask everyone to draw (or paint) a family portrait.

Sit all together at a large table or draw separately and surprise each other.

Don't compete, but emphasise capturing this moment in family history. What does everyone look like now or what hobby characterises them just now?

Keep the portraits in a safe place and repeat this activity once a year to watch artists bud and the family grow.

Years later they will provide warm (and funny) memories for all of you.

More ways of preserving memories

1 Keep a journal of your own, writing down funny things the children say or symbols of growth and understanding.
2 Write letters to your children periodically (maybe on birthdays?) telling them how proud of them you feel.
3 Take lots of photos of them in candid shots. Keep a few in a special hiding place and save for 20 years and then present a chronicle of growth.

4 Keep a box of 'firsts' for 20 years and present at the birth of her first baby. (Include a lock of hair, first drawings, prayers, etc.)
5 Make a quilt history of her life by capturing events in quilt squares. Save until she gets married.
6 Keep some favourite toys after they have been outgrown. Store them safely away until she has children of her own.

Family holiday ideas

Every family needs a holiday EVERY YEAR! Maybe you can't manage a cruise in the Caribbean, but even meagre budgets can manage *something*. (I know.)

Why does your family need a holiday? Because

1 You relax enough to relate differently toward each other (without job pressures, telephone interruptions and routine demands).
2 A change of scenery is psychologically uplifting.
3 You have quality time to give each other.
4 Freedom from demands heightens sensitivity and thus communication.
5 The memories are irreplaceable.

Actually, memories are my strongest argument for family holidays. For I treasure the memories of my family travels as dearly as any in my childhood.

All our children *really* need is TIME. Time spent with us, sharing and playing and praying. Time spent exploring God's beautiful world. Time to BE, together.

Keeping this in mind, then, as you plan your holidays, rules out

frenzied sightseeing
spending all your time with relatives
materialistic entertainment to the
    exclusion of personal relationships
rigid plans for each day (as if
    accomplishment were the goal).

So much for why you need a holiday. On to what you can do cheaply and enjoyably.

1 Join the **Youth Hostel** Association. Accommodation is more than adequate (despite whatever horror stories you may have heard) at £2-3 per night (without breakfast).
2 Try **camping**. No reservations are needed to pitch a tent. And the scenery and peace are free as well. Check your local Tourist Information Centre for a guide to campgrounds in your area.

Another advantage of camping is the teamwork necessary to pitch a tent, cook over a fire or walk another to the loo in the dark.
3 Investigate **farm guesthouses** – especially if you live in the city. Your kids will exult in feeding the animals, and adopting them in the process.

(Note: Look for guidebooks put out by the National Tourist Boards.)
4 Visit a **new area** (or a new country). Enhance the anticipation by writing to tourist bureaux for information, or reading library books about the new area several weeks in advance.

Learn not only the geography but the history of the area as well. Then the trip's educational – but don't tell the kids, they'll just think it's fun!
5 **House-swapping** with friends in another area saves accommodation costs.

(Last year our family swapped with friends on the Isle of Bute (off Scotland) for a week. The house was located right on the bay, had a playroom stocked with toys, a video and even a microwave. Even the rain couldn't spoil that week!)

Be sure to make agreements in advance, though, on use of facilities, food supplies and 'house-rules', to avoid misunderstandings.
6 **Bed and breakfasts** are still my favourite way to holiday. You pay for the service (and wonderful breakfasts) but still retain the home-like quality. We've stayed in many bed and breakfasts and never found a 'loser' yet. All have been different, but all clean and eager for our comfort.

(Note: B & B guides are also put out by the National Tourist Boards.)
7 Stay with **friends** or **relatives** if you can afford the holiday no other way. But do not give more attention to others than to your own family members. (Perhaps a word of explanation in advance to your relatives might be in order. And then be willing to reciprocate for their family.)

Youth Hostel Association addresses

England and Wales:
Trevelyan House
8 St Stephen's Hill
St Albans
Herts A11 2DY

Northern Ireland:
56 Bradbury Place
Belfast BT7 1RU

Republic of Ireland:
39 Mountjoy Square
Dublin 1

Scotland:
7 Glebe Crescent
Stirling FK8 2JA

Christian House Exchange Fellowship
Karakorum
Sunnyfield Lane
Up Hatherley
Cheltenham
Glos. GL51 6JE
Attn: Mr Peter Worsley

Holidays that nurture spirits as well as bodies

What are your options?

1 Royal Week, Spring Harvest and more special family weeks take place in England every year. They are designed to provide entire families with an experience of Christian community, worship and recreation. Other countries hold their own brand of summer family activities. What better way to holiday?

Consider taking your family to a Christian special event week. Then you don't have to worry about the kids being bored or influenced wrongly.
2 Scripture Union camps for children offer more than you might think. How about a sail around the Hebrides for your teenager? Ask your pastor how you can contact your local SU branch.

3 Christian retreat centres abound. Check out a copy of the *UK Christian Handbook* in your local library for a full listing. There's one on Jersey, and even on Iona (Scotland) for a real 'get-away-from-it-all'.
4 Christian hotels also abound. There you can be sure of a healthy atmosphere for your children.

There's also a castle functioning as a Christian centre in **Northern Ireland** and one in **Wales**.

Castle Erin Christian
Endeavour Guest
House
Castle Erin Road
Portrush
Co. Antrim
BT56 8DH
N. Ireland
Attn: Miss M. Workman

Bodlondeb Castle
Church Walks
Llandudno
Gwynedd
LL30 2HH
Wales
Attn: Mr C. Appleton

5 **Christian Travel International Ltd.**, of London, specialises in flights for 'all in the Lord's work'. Another (**Highway Holidays Ltd.**, in Salisbury) specialises in pilgrimages to the Holy Land. Support Christian firms when you need their services.

Scrap book memories

Chronicle each year's family events in a scrapbook. Buy any variety of album. Then keep literally every scrap to record the year of togetherness.

Keep:

ticket stubs from train trips and concerts, or programmes

cards (especially handmade ones) from birthdays and holidays
photographs from even ordinary events
pressed flowers or butterflies found on walks
certificates or rewards
prized drawings by children
postcards from places you've visited
ANYTHING that calls up pleasant memories

Mystery trips

For a special birthday, an attempt to cheer up a family member, or for no special occasion, plan a mystery trip.

1 Choose a destination that will particularly delight one family member.
2 Make necessary arrangements for lodging (if needed), car maintenance, meals, tickets, etc.
3 Plan a departure time and instruct everyone how to dress appropriately.
4 Take the family to this location and then announce the intentions of the mystery trip.
5 Read *Maisie's Mystery Tour* to the children on the way. (*Maisie's Mystery Tour* by Aileen Patterson, Byway Books, 1984.)

Memories aren't all that hard to make . . .

Moving house is hard on kids too

Moving house must be one of life's most challenging feats. So much to remember in getting ready and so much adjusting once you're there. Parents think it's hard on them, but children may fare worse, since they don't possess well-developed coping skills.

What can you do to minimise the stress and avoid creating a bad memory for your children? Well, we've moved several times now and I can only suggest a few tricks we've tried.

1 Allow children to play with friends up until the last possible moment. Don't involve them in the mechanics of packing unless absolutely necessary.
2 If toys must be weeded out (as ours were when moving from one continent to another) allow the children to choose. Explain that you cannot take them all. Then suggest they give some (of their choosing) to the Salvation Army or a needy children's home. Or perhaps it might be meaningful to give a favourite toy to a best friend before moving.
3 If possible, send them to visit grandparents the last day or two so they don't have to see their rooms barren and empty. It avoids some of the grief process and allows them to remember the house furnished and home-like instead.

4 Try not to let yourself get so involved with moving that you don't allow for quality time with each child. They mustn't feel as if they are losing Mum or Dad, too.

5 Go out to eat or provide some special event the day you actually move into the new house. The togetherness will make up for some of the stress caused by sleeping the first night in a new place.

6 Spend as long as necessary at bedtime to make each child feel secure in a new room.

7 Let children make suggestions for the arrangement and decoration of their new rooms. Help them make it their own.

8 Spend time early on helping your children get acquainted with neighbouring children. The sooner they make new friends, the sooner everyone will settle into acceptance and security in a new place.

9 If others don't make the first move, invite new neighbours over to get acquainted – especially those with children of similar ages to yours.

Do all you can to minimise the stress on your children and your stress will lessen as well.

Parents need treats too

If you want secure, well-adjusted children, then you, as parents, must be secure in your marital relationship.

Children feel most secure in a family where Mum and Dad are happy with each other. When Mum and Dad hug and kiss in front of children, they know that the home is stable and love reigns over all problems that may arise.

Couples must nurture their relationship – must even place their marriage as first priority. But nurture takes time. Parents need to plan a time each day to 'debrief' and talk with their spouse about what they are thinking and how they are feeling. Couples who neglect this essential, daily communication, soon find themselves at odds and the children suffer from the tension.

Children know when parents are irritable and at odds with each other. You don't do them any favours by staying with them, to the exclusion of time alone as a couple. The best way for parents to stay in touch is to take regular time away together. A weekend away every three to six months should provide ample time to unload repressed feelings and regain the joys of intimacy.

Your children will not resent your going without them if you explain to them how much you love each other and that Mum (or Dad) needs your attention too. They will see, when you return, the benefits of relaxation alone together. (Little ones who cry must not be allowed to ruin such a necessity.)

Whom God has joined together, let not child or business tear asunder . . .

First or last day of school celebrations

To motivate children in their educational process, be sure to celebrate their progress. It may only be the beginning of another school year, but you can turn that into a warm memory of Mum and Dad's moral support.

Plan a special event or even a party to commemorate school opening (or closing, if that suits you better). Ideas?

1 Organise a neighbourhood barbecue in your garden for all your child's friends the day before school begins. You plan the food and let them organise games, relays and races.
2 Hold an annual family picnic the first evening of school. Be sure to have the same menu and use the same location. Encourage children to set goals for the school year and promise (nonmaterial) rewards for the accomplishment of those goals.
3 Take the children out to lunch the last day of school (since they usually finish by noon on the last day). Go somewhere they choose, and go every year to the same place to cement memories.

15

4 Plan an annual outing to the zoo, favourite beach or other family favourite the last day before school begins (or the day after school closes for the summer).

5 Make an event of shopping for school clothes for the coming year. Go to a different city or farther than necessary to add fun to an otherwise routine trip. Over lunch, talk about fears or joys pertaining to the coming year.

These celebrations are particularly helpful to the less-than-eager student and certainly aren't scorned by the eager beaver. Besides, the memories are worth the effort even if it has no bearing on their schooling whatever.

Educational trips near your house

What educational outings can you plan near your home? Well, obviously some places are better suited for educational outings than others. But you can make an educational trip of otherwise routine things.

1 Visit a different type of church. Angela had a best friend who was Jewish and found it very interesting to go to synagogue with Susan on Friday nights. Do a bit of study, if necessary, so you can answer questions that may arise on other faiths.

2 Take the children to an orchestral concert, an opera, or ballet if you're lucky enough to be near them. You may think they won't appreciate it, but you'll be wrong. They may not choose opera over the zoo, but the experience will broaden them as individuals.

3 Art galleries are loved by children – even if they don't understand the finer details and meanings implied in the paintings. By all means, take even young children to a good art gallery.

4 Nature centres abound – even if you live in the city. Most areas have a nature centre of some sort. It may not be a full-fledged zoo, but children love all forms of animal life and won't complain.

5 Take them to any and all factories or businesses in which they are allowed. Try to catch university astronomy department open evenings or any other unusual event you can find for them to visit.

6 The local fire department is always a great thrill for children. Call ahead to ask when would be a good time.

Virtually anything can be made educational if you just take the time to explain to your children the details behind everyday realities. Such as how petrol is stored in tanks underground (as well as how oil is pumped from underground initially): how cheese is made: or what happens to the wool on the sheep they see on the hills.

Making people memories

Phil and I were on a bus for a 12-hour trip recently and began talking about the influence outsiders in our home had on us.

Phil grew up as a minister's son and it was routine to have someone in after church on Sunday evenings. He knew, as a child, many well-known Christians for they had eaten together at his home. And their influence has had lasting effects on his life and thinking.

We have adopted this practice and volunteer to have speakers, missionaries, etc., in our home. We enjoy their company and learn from others serving God.

Bu we also feel it is an excellent means of exposing our children to God via his people. Their lives of love and service to God often say things our children would rather not hear from us. And they begin to understand that this business of following God is not just Mum and Dad's idea, but a lot of other people believe in it too.

Make sure you don't overlook this means of educating your children in the Christian life.

Christmas baking

One of the memories which springs quickly to my mind from my childhood is Christmas baking.

Mum and I would spend hours in the kitchen (from about November on) making fudge, special Christmas biscuits and various sweets. The time we spent together was enjoyable and still evokes warm memories.

Why did we bake so much for a family of three? To give away. We gave goodies to the postman, the neighbours, the minister and various friends – just for the love of giving. (And Christmas wasn't the only time of year. Mum and I were often found cooking for others who were ill, moving house or any number of needs.)

Here, I learned not only to bake, but the joy of giving and the joy of doing something with Mum. Why not begin this family tradition in your house and bake up some memories for your children?

Picnics

Another of Phil's favourite family memories is picnics. Coming from a large family, it was a celebration just to have everyone together for a picnic.

He and I have certainly made use of this memory-maker for our children. We use any excuse to eat outdoors. Never mind the weather or the perfection of the surroundings. Our favourite place to picnic is on a large rock which juts out into the sea next to the (ruined) castle. Or we walk down the Lade Braes and sit by a chattering stream. We've even picnicked in a car, rather than give up our picnic when it rained on our plans.

You don't need elaborate food. I am always amazed at how my girls love sandwiches. They'd rather have a sandwich by the sea than steak at home. Anything will do. Just take it outside.

So the next nice evening you find free, scrap the idea of cooking and take everyone to some outdoor spot and picnic a memory!

Books for making memories

Let's Make a Memory, **Shirley Dobson** and **Gloria Gaither**, Word Books, 1983. UK Christian Handbook, **Ed. Peter Brierley**, MarcEurope Books, 1987.

2 Family nights

I recently read an essay by G.K. Chesterton called 'Foes of the Family' (in *The Well and the Shallows*, Sheed and Ward, 1935, p. 147). He concluded that capitalism was destroying the family (his view in 1935). Why? Because

1 The pursuit of money took people from their homes too long.
2 Authority was transferred from parent to employer.
3 Life consisted of commercial goals, rather than family ones.

And isn't he right? Don't job priorities determine our lifestyle and family life, in particular? Then, in the time we have left, we often neglect family time owing to church or other obligations.

I believe God's priority list to be

1 God first
2 Family
3 Job
4 Everything else.

One way of giving family priority is to set aside 'family nights'. This simply means keeping one night a week inviolable by everyone else. It gives a night to relax and enjoy the company of those most important to you. Let me suggest several rules to keep family nights 'family only':

1 Refuse all other invitations for (Thursdays).
2 Take the phone off the hook.

3 If anyone drops by, explain politely that it's not a convenient time for company and set another time for them to return.
4 Keep the TV off. Family commmunication is the goal.
5 Keep set times, such as 6-8 p.m., for togetherness. After that, family members may pursue personal goals (maybe in the same room for continued togetherness).
6 Begin with a realistic schedule for family nights. If every week will become a burden, make it every other Thursday. (Don't begin a weekly routine and then drop it.)

Several family night ideas are suggested in this chapter to get you started. But you will want to tailor them to your likes and your children's ages.

The following schedule is only an approximation.

5.45-6.15 Supper
6.15-6.30 Family devotions
6.30-7.30 Playing games (or planned activity)
7.30-8.00 Reading aloud

Family Nights are also a good time for family conferences. (Assuming your children are five and older, they'll have an opinion on most everything.) Discuss holiday plans or discipline or family night activities *on* family nights – in the warm atmosphere of togetherness.

(*Listen* to your children's ideas. Sometimes their ideas are better than ours. And even if you can't indulge all their whims, give them a reason why not (besides 'that's a stupid idea').)

Books to read aloud

Adams, Richard, *Watership Down,* Penguin, 1972

Alcott, Louisa May, *Little Men,* Penguin, 1983.

Barrie, J.M., *Peter Pan,* Collins, 1988.

Baum, L. Frank, *The Wizard of Oz,* Penguin, 1985.

Blyton, Enid, *Fire on Treasure Island,* Hodder, 1974 (and other books by the same author).

Bond, Michael, *A Bear Called Paddington,* Collins, 1958 (and several sequels).

Burnett, Francis Hogsdon, *Little Lord Fauntleroy,* J.M. Dent & Sons, 1962.

The Children's Bible, Hamlyn, 1964.

Corbett, W.J., *The Song of Pentecost,* Methuen, 1982.

Curtis, Philip, *The Complete Borrowers Stories,* Penguin, 1983.

Dicks, Terrence, *T.R. Afloat,* Piccadilly, 1986 (one of a series of T.R. Bear books).

Grahame, Kenneth, *The Wind in the Willows,* Methuen, 1959.

A Kaleidoscope of Fairies and Fables (stories of **Hans Christian Anderson, Aesop, Kipling,** and **the Brothers Grimm**) Hamlyn, 1988.

Keene, Carolyn, *The Secret of Mirror Bay,* Collins, 1972 (one of a series of Nancy Drew children's mysteries).

Kipling, Rudyard, *The Jungle Book,* MacMillan, 1983.

Lewis, C.S., *The Chronicles of Narnia* (a series of seven books), Collins, 1953.

Manning-Sanders, Ruth, ed., *Folk and Fairy Tales,* Methuen, 1978.

Milne, A.A., *Now We Are Six,* Methuen, 1987.

Patterson, Aileen, *Maisie Goes to Glasgow* (one of a series of Maisie the cat books), Three Hill Books, 1988.

Potter, Beatrix, *The Tale of Flopsy Bunnies,* Frederick Warne, 1987 (and many other titles).

Powers, Mala, *Follow the Star,* Hodder, 1980.

Sewell, Anna, *Black Beauty,* Penguin, 1954.

Stevenson, Robert L., *Treasure Island,* Canongate, 1988.

Tolkien, J.R.R., *The Hobbit,* Unwin, 1951.

Utley, Alison, *Little Grey Rabbit's Party,* Collins, 1983 (and other titles).

White, E.B., *Charlotte's Web,* Penguin, 1963.

White, T.H., *The Sword in the Stone,* Collins, 1938.

Wilder, Laura Ingalls, *The Little House on the Prairie,* Penguin, 1964 (and sequels).

Wyss, J.D., *Swiss Family Robinson,* Penguin, 1986.

Winnie-the-Pooh birthday party

For a unique and enjoyable Family Night, celebrate Winnie-the-Pooh's birthday. (Pooh turned 60 years old in March of 1986. Give the old man a party!)

1 Bake a Pooh-shaped cake.
2 Have a Pooh-look-alike contest.
3 Borrow a Pooh record from the local library.
4 Read a Pooh story after dinner.
5 Don't forget to have honey for tea.

Any excuse for celebration will do!

Queen's birthday party

21 April (actual day) or 12 June (official date)
Similarly, you can celebrate God and country by throwing a birthday party for the Queen. (You'll need to invite her well in advance.)

1 Supply the kids with paper to create a large Union Jack.
2 Bake a cake (roughly) shaped like your country (or maybe Buckingham Palace?). Of course, the children will decorate it.
3 Plan a simple party supper menu.
4 Hang streamers and balloons.
5 Sing 'God Save the Queen' before cutting the cake.

6 Assign Dad the task of finding some humorous or unusual historical event to tell.
7 Play 'national' trivia over your tea.

Supper discussion starters

Do you ever feel as if your supper conversation is less than helpful? I do. So I brainstormed for topic ideas for initiating healthy discussions. Hope they're helpful at your supper table.

1 The best thing about our family is . . .
2 The thing I'd really like to change in this family is . . .
3 If our family could do *anything*, I wish it could be . . .
4 I wish our church . . .
5 I'd like to help . . .
6 When I grow up, I hope I . . .
7 My favourite Bible story is . . .
8 For our holiday, I'd like to go to . . .
9 If I had a million pounds, I'd . . .
10 I wish I could be more like X (family member) because . . .
11 I like the way Jesus . . .
12 If I ran our government . . .
13 The greatest person who ever lived was X because . . .
14 In this book I'm reading, I learned . . .
15 I am concerned about X because . . .

Wholemeal buttermilk pancakes

¾ pint buttermilk (add a dessertspoon of vinegar to ordinary milk)
3 tablespoons vegetable oil
1 egg
4 oz. wholemeal flour
3 oz. plain flour
1½ teaspoons baking powder
1 teaspoon bicarbonate of soda
½ teaspoon salt

Stir all ingredients together until smooth. Fry in a hot, lightly oiled frying pan, or on a griddle.

Optional additions to batter:

cooked apples, banana slices, pineapple chopped nuts and raisins

Toppings we usually use:

fruit jams
natural sugarless fruit preserves maple syrup (if you can afford it)
any fruits and fruit sauces.

As long as you don't pour too much golden syrup or other 'sticky' on it, it's a cheap, quick and healthy supper that my kids beg for.

It's also an easy recipe for 10 year-olds-plus to make on their own.

Pennsylvania Dutch Funnel Cakes

3 eggs
1 pt. milk
2 oz. sugar
½ teaspoon salt
2 tablespoons baking powder
12-14 oz. plain flour

Beat the batter until smooth, adding only as much flour as needed. Batter should be thin enough to run through a funnel. Drop batter from funnel into deep, hot fat. Design spirals and fancy shapes by criss-crossing while controlling the funnel spout with your finger. Coat in icing sugar and eat while still hot.

Your kids will love them!

Instead of TV list

Make an 'Instead of TV list' of activities for the family. Be sure every family member contributes ideas and that suggestions don't exclude family members (such as Scrabble, which a four-year-old couldn't play).

Write the suggestions on strips of paper and place in a box (which the children can decorate).

Then on family nights when no specific activity is planned, children can take turns pulling a 'surprise activity' for the evening from the box.

Buttermilk Pancakes

Another Family Night favourite at the Bences is making a meal of buttermilk pancakes.

I use a healthy wholemeal pancake recipe and I sometimes double the recipe to have some left for heating on hurried school mornings.

This amount serves four, with none to spare for breakfasts.

Going Dutch

Pennsylvania Dutch Funnel Cakes are well known and loved in the eastern half of the United States.

The Pennsylvania Dutch themselves would make a great topic for further investigation. They are a very religious group who came originally from Europe. Fleeing religious persecution (in the 1600s), they settled in various locations in the United States, but the great majority settled in eastern Pennsylvania.

They refuse to use electricity or drive cars, using horses and buggies instead. They are nearly all farmers and, therefore, great cooks as well.

Funnel cakes are even sold in booths at fairs, etc. Now, with this recipe, you can make your own!

A Mexican evening

Some Family Nights, you might want to concentrate on other countries. It really doesn't take that much preparation. Simply choose a country

---

Kathy's Vegetable Tortillas – **a family favourite**

Tortilla dough (serves 4)

| 8 oz. plain flour | 2 oz. vegetable shortening |
| 1 teaspoon salt | ¼ pint lukewarm water |

Mix flour, salt and shortening into crumbly pastry, then add the water and work to a doughy consistency. *Chill overnight*, **covered. Next day, divide the dough into 10 small balls, and roll each as thin as possible on a floured board. Fry quickly (about 20 seconds) in a lightly oiled frying pan or griddle, turning once. Set aside.**

Filling

Set oven to gas mark 5, 375°F

5 fl. oz. plain yoghurt	1 tin red kidney beans
1 small tin cooked	1 teaspoon chili powder
spinach (or frozen,	1 teaspoon cumin
but it costs more)	14 oz. tin chopped tomatoes
1 small tin sweetcorn	cheddar cheese, grated

everyone would enjoy learning about – Mexico for instance.

1 Check to see what's available at the local library. (Often the young readers' section has travel books on just the level you'd need for this.)
2 Glance through the book and mark down page numbers of information you think would most interest your children.

3 If your library lends records or tapes, check for Mexican music as well.
4 Buy ingredients for the following menu and make the tortilla (pronounced 'tor-tea-a') dough the day before.
5 If you happen to have straw hats for gardening, wear them. And tell the children to dress in their brightest reds and yellows.

To make the kidney beans 'Mexican', fry them quickly in a hot lightly oiled pan and mash them with a potato masher. Stir together all the ingredients except the tomatoes and cheese, then spoon some filling onto each tortilla. Roll up the filled tortillas, and place close together in a casserole dish. Pour over the chopped tomatoes and sprinkle the cheese on top. Bake for 30 minutes.

It's truly worth the effort. Make it a family project to prepare if you want help. Then you could read about Mexico while waiting for them to cook.

Accompany with a tropical fruit salad of pineapple, coconut, kiwi and oranges.   *Olé!*

---

3 Holidays and traditions add spice to family life

Holidays and traditions are so intertwined as to become inseparable in my mind. So, if in reading this chapter you think I've confused them, remember this: 'She's not only confused them, she's made them synonymous!'

That is because I am still a child at heart and I love any reason to celebrate! Holidays or traditions, it makes no difference to me, let's celebrate something! Better yet, let's celebrate life!

There's a delightful song called 'Lord of the Dance' by Sydney Carter, which captures this idea of celebrating for me.

> Dance, then wherever you may be,
> I am the Lord of the dance, said he,
> And I'll lead you all wherever you
>   may be,
> And I'll lead you all in the Dance,
>   said he.

> v.1 I danced in the morning
> When the world was begun,
> And I danced in the moon
> And the stars and the sun;
> And I came down from heaven
> And I danced on the earth,
> At Bethlehem
> I had my birth.

> v.4 I danced on a Friday
> when the sky turned black:
> It's hard to dance
> With the devil on your back.

> They buried my body
> And they thought I'd gone;
> But I am the dance,
> And I still go on.
>   *Faith, Folk and Nativity.*
>   Galliard Ltd.

It may take some practice, but consider celebration as an approach to life, not just for your children (though they'll blossom), but for yourself. Joy is its own reward.

My approach to holidays and traditions in this chapter will be seasonal, working right through the year for easier reference.

Obviously, all of these ideas aren't appropriate for all families. So if one fails, try another. Hopefully they'll provide a beginning point for you to mould your own traditions of celebration.

Candlemas celebration at home

2 February   Candlemas falls on 2 February, the fortieth day after Christmas. It represents the day Jesus' parents would have taken him to the Temple for presentation. This Jewish custom is similar to our tradition of dedicating or baptising babies.

The temples used lots of candles for

lighting. Later, churches developed the custom of remembering Candlemas by blessing a year's supply of candles for the church.

You can celebrate Candlemas at home in a couple of ways.

1 Retell the story of Jesus' dedication at the Temple. Light lots of candles and choose one taper to watch. Then let the children stay up until that one candle burns all the way down and flickers out. A family night would suit well since you could do other things together while watching the candle burn down.

2 You can commemorate the dedication or baptism of your children when they were young. Bring out pictures and certificates to explain to your children why you, as parents, dedicated them to God, for his use.

2 February happens to be our anniversary, but it's also the date of a very funny custom in the United States: it is called Groundhog's Day. A groundhog is a small badger-like animal that hibernates underground in the winter.

On 2 February, in Punkxatawny, Pennsylvania, people get up very early to watch a hole where they know a groundhog is hibernating. If the groundhog comes out on a sunny day and sees his shadow, he runs back into his hole, thus signifying six more weeks of winter. If he comes out on a cloudy day (and sees no shadow) it supposedly means an early spring. People around the country enjoy hearing 'Punkxatawny Phil's' prediction.

(Whether the groundhog forecasts spring accurately is open to debate, but it's a fun custom.)

St Valentine's Day

14 February   Have you ever wondered about the origin of Valentine's Day? According to legend, Valentine was the name of a young priest during the time when the Roman Emperor, Claudius, banned marriage.

Valentine secretly married as many young couples as he could before the law went into effect. He knew what sorrow this law would cause so he helped in the only way he could. But Claudius had him killed for his kindness. In 468 AD, the Church declared Valentine a saint. St Valentine's Day has been celebrated on 14 February ever since.

Even before this, the Romans had a festival dedicated to love and to two mythological gods, Pan (the god of nature) and Juno (the goddess of women and marriage). It was there that drawings of cupids originated.

I must confess I have always loved St Valentine's Day. It brings back warm memories of my Daddy bringing sweets to me and my Mom, of guessing the identity of secret admirers, of an excuse for the expression of affection between friends.

I still buy red sugar paper and paper doilies and make Valentine's cards with my girls. I always make one for Phil, even though he takes a rather less interested view of this day. He knows better than to buy me chocolates (I am always dieting) but he also knows I'm hoping for some small expression of his love.

Why is this day special? Because we all need to hear again and again that we are loved. We shouldn't need a holiday to remind us, but St Valentine's Day certainly makes it easier for shy people (or those who get too busy to say 'I love you'). Make sure you tell each member of your family EVERY DAY that you love them. And do milk St Valentine's Day for all the fun and love you can get out of it:

1 Bake heart-shaped biscuits or cakes.
2 Colour anything and everything red!
3 Make a Valentine's card for each family member.
4 Dress up in Sunday best and have high tea that evening. (Heart-shaped sandwiches, biscuits, mints, red napkins and anything else that says 'love'.)
5 Make small red hearts and tape them to your windows, doors, etc.
6 Make Valentine's cards for some elderly neighbours or friends. Then visit them to deliver Valentines and heart-shaped biscuits.
7 Make peppermint creams cut out in heart shapes.
8 Write new 'Roses are Red' love poems for each family member.
9 Do some unexpected kindness for each family member (do a job they hate, or some thoughtful extra).

Spring into Spring!

Spring cannot be ignored, after months of cold, dreary weather and fidgety children. Use every excuse to celebrate nature and life in general.

1 Plant every kind of seed you want to see flourishing around you.
2 Consider this year planting vegetables as well. Actually, they require less tending than flowers.
3 Take walks often, watching bulbs peeping out of the ground and identifying each new flower as it comes into bloom.
4 Plan nature projects and begin anticipating spring earlier than usual.
5 Read your children spring and nature poems. (Try William Blake's 'The Lamb' (see below) and others from his 'Songs of Innocence'. Many of them centre around the seasons and nature.)
6 Visit a farm to see baby animals and talk about the miracle of growth and God's creation.

'The Lamb' by William Blake

Little Lamb, who made thee?
Dost thou know who made thee?
Gave thee life, and bid thee feed?
By the stream and o'er the mead;
Gave thee clothing of delight,
Softest clothing, woolly, bright:
Gave thee such a tender voice,
Making all the vales rejoice?
　Little lamb, who made thee?
　Little lamb, who made thee?

　Little lamb, I'll tell thee;
　Little lamb, I'll tell thee;
He is called by thy name,
For He calls Himself a lamb.
He is meek, and He is mild,

He became a little child,
I a child, and thou a lamb,
We are called by His name.
   Little lamb, God bless thee!
   Little lamb, God bless thee!

St Patrick's Day

17 March   Why do we celebrate St Patrick's dying day? Until recently, I didn't know and maybe you aren't so clear on your facts either. His life makes a great story to tell your children.

According to tradition, a young man named Patrick lived in the fifth century in Ireland. He was a godly young man who became a leader among the people.

He disliked the Irish practice of worshipping the return of the sun in the spring. So he transformed their pagan celebration into one with Christian meaning. He suggested that the bonfires on Easter Eve could represent lighting the way for Christ through the underworld (before His victory over death on Easter morning).

Another contribution he made was to teach Latin to the Irish clergy (since most of them couldn't read) and he also founded many monasteries.

He often used the shamrock as an illustration of the Trinity – Father, Son and Holy Spirit (three, but all one).

There's even a legend that he drove all the snakes out of Ireland. But whether you believe that story or not, it is true that when he died, the people mourned and made Patrick a saint, and 17 March a national holiday.

Suggest to your children that they might someday be famous for their Christian lives if they follow God's plan. We never know upon what adventure He may lead us!

Your children may want to do more reading on St Patrick or draw shamrocks or colour their milk green on St Patrick's Day. If possible, you might even light a bonfire and burn off all the brush from last year's garden.

Mothers' Day

The tradition of Mothers' Day is older than I thought: the custom began in the Middle Ages. Young people apprenticed to some trade usually lived far from home (far, when you had to travel on foot). They were allowed one Sunday a year to go home and visit their families. This day became a holiday and was also known as Simnel Cake Day – on which they ate simnel cakes, of course. I'm not sure I can come up with many new suggestions for celebrating Mothers' Day other than the ancient custom of baking a simnel cake (see below).

Have every family member help with the baking and maybe even pitch in and give Mum a day (or two!) off housework too. And don't forget to tell her you love her in some way *other* than buying something. She'll appreciate thoughtful ideas more than shop-bought cards and sweets.

Lent observances and customs

The word 'Lent' comes from an old English word for spring which means 'lengthen'. This was, of course, related to the days lengthening.

It is customarily a time for self-examination and additional spiritual disciplines (such as fasting and extra prayer times), as we reconsider the death of Christ on the cross.

Many churches suggest some type of fast during the 40 days of Lent. In days past, people decided to give up luxuries in eating, like eggs, meat, milk and butter. This explains the custom of making pancakes before Lent in Britain and pretzels in France.

In other countries people confessed their sins and tried to give up old habits which were displeasing to God.

In France, Lenten calendars were shaped like a nun. She had seven feet. One was turned over for each of the seven weeks of Lent.

In America (in New Orleans, Louisiana, to be exact), a huge festival is held just before the beginning of Lent. The Mardi Gras, as it is called, features huge parades, all-night revels in costumes and masks, and entertainment that lasts for ten days prior to Lent. Rio de Janeiro (Brazil) holds similar carnivals preceding Lent.

Simnel Cake

Set oven to gas mark 2, 300°F

6 oz. butter	1 teaspoon cinnamon
6 oz. Demerara sugar	1 teaspoon mixed spice
3 eggs	1 lb. currants
8 oz. self-raising flour	4 oz. mixed peel

Mix ingredients. Spoon half of cake mixture into bottom of tin. On top of that, lay a circle of marzipan, then the rest of the cake mixture. Bake for about 3 hours.

Cool. Then spoon a bit of warm jam on top of cake and cover that with another circle of marzipan. Then form 12 small balls of marzipan and place equally distant around the top of the cake. (These represent the 12 disciples.) Brush with beaten egg yolk and grill a few seconds to glaze. Then fill centre with water icing and decorate.

You and your family can choose any of these ways of celebrating Lent. Or you might like to re-enact the Passover (see below) to prepare for the coming of spring and Easter.

Passover re-enactment

Sometime during Lent (ideally in Holy Week), conduct a family study of the Exodus and Passover (see Exodus 12).

After the children have learned the story, do a family play of the Passover as authentically as you can.

What you'll need to do:

1 Clear the chairs from the dining room (the Israelites ate standing).
2 Prepare the appropriate food (see below).
3 Dress appropriately for travel. (Wear your coats.)
4 Have Dad read through the story before telling the children (as Scripture commands the Jews to do forever).
5 After your 'play' is completed, sit to eat the rest of your meal (perhaps only vegetables and fruit to remain authentic). Then discuss how millions of Jews all over the wold still celebrate the Passover near the same time we Christians celebrate Easter.

Food for Passover   Pieces of roasted lamb, seasoned with bitter herbs. 'Bitter herbs' in the Bible usually meant chicory, lettuce, peppermint and dandelion. These were served in a sauce of pounded nuts and fruits in vinegar. Something different on your menu . . .
Dates, figs, dried fruits
Pitta bread

Easter

It's unfortunate that Easter receives less attention in our lives than Christmas.

Christmas, while important, should not be treated more seriously than Easter. We may argue that it isn't, but our lifestyles speak otherwise. Ask yourself: which holiday do you spend more time preparing?

Easter must also compete with our excitement over the joys of spring, so let's try to incorporate both into our Easter celebrations. Every flower or chick or new lamb brings cause for rejoicing over the miracle of life, the triumph of spring over winter. And that can lead discussion directly on to the greater miracle: Christ's triumph of life over death.

Relate every aspect of life to Christ's rule over all the earth. Read Psalm 104, which depicts the glories of His reign over all creation. Try to transmit to your children the wonder of resurrection, be it Christ's body or a lowly seed.

1 Plant bulbs (the autumn before) which bloom in early spring.
2 Consider keeping a rabbit, or check to see if your local agricultural school has eggs incubating – arrange for your children to see chicks hatch.
3 Plant a shrub or tree at Easter as a symbol of the triumph of life over death.
4 Make a project of a family Easter sunrise service. Let each family member help prepare and take part in your

Hot Cross buns

Set oven to gas mark 7, 425°F

8 oz. plain flour	**1 egg**
¼ teaspoon mixed spice	**3 oz. currants**
¼ pint milk	**½ oz. chopped peel**
½ oz. yeast	**1 tablespoon sugar**
1½ oz. castor sugar	**boiled with 1 tablespoon**
2 oz. butter	**milk to glaze**

Warm the milk and yeast until dissolved. Let cool slightly and mix with rest of ingredients. Let rise for an hour and a half in a warm place. Knock down and let rise 30 minutes more. Form into eight balls and let rise another 15 minutes. Run a sharp knife across each bun to form the cross (or make a cross with icing when baked and cooled). Bake for 15 minutes, cool, and glaze.

service. (Be sure to hold it outside in some scenic spot.)

5 Make a tradition of baking hot cross buns together (see above) for eating outside after your sunrise service.

6 Or hold a family communion service on Good Friday (or Easter Eve) as you think about the passion and death of Christ.

7 Include the 'Easter Bunny' for small children if you like, but keep the Easter eggs for days leading up to Easter, and reserve worship and celebration for Easter Day.

Maybe you might like to try adding these customs to your Easter celebrations this year.

Holy Week   In Eastern Europe, people greet each other with three kisses (to represent the three crosses and the Trinity).

In Germany and in Sweden huge bonfires are lit. The ancient custom was to light a fire and slaughter animals as praise offerings to the sun god for the return of the sun in the spring. But in Portugal, effigies of Judas are burned on the bonfires on Good Friday. Brazilians stage great parades with young girls dressed as angels. Parades in Seville, Spain, portray biblical stories on huge floats.

Maundy Thursday The word Maundy comes from a Latin word, 'mandatum', meaning command (for it was on this last night with his disciples that Jesus gave them many commands). It was shortened to Maundy but still is celebrated on the Thursday of Holy Week, with communion and solemn thoughts of Christ's death on the morrow (Good Friday). In many places they still hold foot washings, as Jesus did, and give money to the poor.

Good Friday The 'good' in Good Friday originated from 'God's Friday' or 'Holy Friday' (representing the good Christ did for us when he died for us).

Danes call it 'Long Friday' and Europeans call it 'Great Friday'.
In Mexico, Christians wear black to symbolise Christ's suffering on the cross.
Years ago, Europeans wouldn't wash any clothes on Good Friday for they thought blood-stains would appear on the clothing.
Many people plant seeds on Good Friday, believing it to be the only time when the devil can't stop growth.
In Poland, they hold huge passion plays on Good Friday.
In Mexico, Monaco, Italy and South America, colourful processions are held, carrying carved figurines of the chief characters of the Holy Week story in the Bible.

Easter Eve In many countries, candles are carried to the church. There, the candles are lit from the central Paschal candle and then people walk home carrying their lighted candles through the streets.

Easter eggs and bunnies

The first Easter Day was declared in 325 AD. And long before that, pagan spring celebrations used eggs, chicks and hares as symbols of new birth.
The Polish people even tell a story that Mary painted eggs for the boy, Jesus, to hide.
In Greece, they carry a dyed egg in one hand and greet each other on Easter day by knocking the eggs together lightly and saying 'Christ is risen!'
But what of our modern Easter celebration with all its elaborate materialistic preparations? We need to think very carefully about what values we want to convey to our children. Do we want them to remember lavish, materialistic Easter frivolities – or the joy of living, the re-creation of life, spiritual and physical?
I always dye eggs and hide them with my girls but I do NOT buy huge Easter eggs. I usually buy some very small item, perhaps to be worn on Easter Day. This I place at the foot of their beds on Easter morning as I wake them.
I do not buy Easter eggs for five reasons:

1 They are overpriced.
2 The sweets are non-nutritious. Why pay a lot for something worthless to our bodies?
3 With so many people starving, it seems to me wrong to waste money in this way.
4 Well-meaning friends usually give them sweets anyway. (I haven't figured out a polite way to ask them not to.)
5 I want Easter remembered as special days of sunrise services, special dinners with guests, and the resurrection.

Whatever you choose for your family, think it through and question why you spend and think and celebrate as you do. Once you've thought it through, pray about what you want to communicate to your children and ask the Lord to guide you.

Easter Projects

An Easter hare (as it's called in Europe) to make

1 Take a boiled egg and dye or paint it brown (or some fanciful colour if you wish).
2 Paint a face on one end.
3 Glue cotton wool on him here and there.
4 Cut out felt ears and glue on one end of the egg.
5 Put a cotton tail on the other end.
6 Cut small lengths of thread for whiskers and glue around mouth.
7 If you prop him in an Easter arrangement, he will look as if he's standing up.

Naturally decorated eggs   To make interesting foresty designs, wrap an unboiled egg in leaves or small flowers, then wrap in a layer of onion skin. Tie lightly with string to hold in place. Boil eggs 10 minutes and let them cool. Carefully unwrap and enjoy your floral design.

Natural dyes to use:
spinach juice – green
beetroot juice – red
tea – brown
carrot juice – orange
(boiled) onion juice – light yellow

Michaelmas or Harvest celebration

The archangel Michael, with his sword of iron and light (see Revelation 12:7-9), is synonymous with the festival of courage. Michael, conquering his dragon, represents a source of courage to Christians who fight dragons in this world or in their own lives.

Harvest celebrations and Michaelmas fall at the end of September. They consist of festive costumes, plenteous food, music and dancing, in most every country.

In some parts of England, it has long been the custom to eat goose. In the olden days, tenants had to give their lord a goose.

Today, churches celebrate the Harvest season by giving food gifts to those in need, in countries which are suffering under famine.

Think of ways to share your 'harvest' (i.e. wealth) with those in need around you this harvest season.

Hallowe'en meditation

31 October Use Hallowe'en as an excuse to talk about the invisible masks we wear, how we hide behind them and play pretend games that are dishonest. (Such as pretending we have forgiven someone when we haven't, or pretending we are busy so we don't have to help someone else.)

Offer honesty and openness as God's alternatives. For example: God became visible in the life of Jesus to show who He is and what He likes.

Each family member could resolve not to wear a particular mask they've formerly hidden behind. You might want to end your discussion with a simple prayer such as this:

Dear God,
Help me to live openly and honestly with others as I'd have them act toward me.

Amen.

Day of Thanksgiving

Adopt a new tradition by adapting the American Day of Thanksgiving for your family.

Set aside a (Sun)day towards the end of November as Thanksgiving Day at your house. You might want to invite some people for whom you are thankful, to join you.

Plan a special meal, with or without a turkey (the traditional main course), but prepare the house and the meal for celebration. Children might make posters or collages showing things for which they are thankful.

Assign someone the job of choosing a psalm of thanksgiving to read. Assign everyone the task of thinking about which person and which event they were most thankful for in the past year.

Then eat, drink and be thankful!

Christmas

One gorgeous Indian woman (Hindu)
Three Malawi students of medicine, and
One American economics PhD student
all joined our family of four for Christmas Day church services and dinner.

And only one of them was a churchgoer or remotely interested in Christianity. They came because Christmas is NOT a time to be alone – no matter what your faith, or lack of it.

And they listened as we read Luke 2 aloud and they prayed as we prayed over the meal. We had stimulating dinner conversation and a delightful day getting acquainted. I'm sure our family will cherish this cosmopolitan

Christmas Day memory forever. (This idea holds equally true at Easter or other family celebrations.)

Inviting others for Christmas Day

If Christmas really means a time of giving, consider giving to others what no money can buy – the memory of a Christmas celebration with *your* family. Check around your neighbourhood, church, or with acquaintances, to find those who have nowhere to spend Christmas Day. There are more lonely people than you think.

What about elderly friends? Or foreign students at a nearby university? Or divorcees or single parents – or just singles? Sometimes time and money prevent even those with family from travelling. And you can make their Christmas meaningful by including others in your 'family'.

The added benefit is the memories you'll make for your children. Chances are they'll be doing the same thing in 20 years.

DID YOU KNOW . . .
that in Norway even the animals are remembered with treats at Christmas? And no hunting or fishing is allowed during the Christmas season so the animals may dwell in peace. What a nice idea!

Christmas Eve magic

Delightful legends about Christmas Eve abound. One says that at midnight animals kneel to pray and receive the gift of speech to tell the story of Jesus' birth.

Another claims that flowers bloom at midnight, bent trees miraculously straighten, and evergreens blossom in the forest to greet the Christ child.

Whatever you may or may not believe of Christmas legends, don't lose your child-like wonder at the miracle of Christmas.

When I was young, my Daddy used to take me outside on starry Christmas Evenings to look for the natal star. I always expected to see it and was never disappointed. In watching the starry heavens with Daddy, I completely forgot about a particular star. But I still cherish warm memories of the closeness of God and of Daddy.

Choose whatever you like, but plan something special for Christmas Eve so your children will remember it with awe and joy.

You may (with older children) want to make a habit of going to a midnight service in some church nearby. (I used to go to a midnight service in a different church on Christmas Eve and it *made* my whole Christmas magical with the lateness of the hour, the lovely music, the different tradition of this church from mine, and the quiet streets upon returning home. It truly seemed a night of miracles.)

Even if your children are young, they can take a nap earlier in the day and then stay up. The experience is worth every bit of extra trouble.

Magical Christmas evenings, of course, require completing all your work ahead of time. Don't let this special time become merely a last-minute frenzy. If it isn't done by then, forget it.

You might even like to talk with your children about the Wise Men beginning their journey as they see the star and speculate on its meaning. The legends about the Magi tell us:
Melchior was a maths genius. His gift of gold represents wisdom.
Balthazar was an astronomer. His gift of frankincense represents compassion.
Caspar was a doctor of medicine. His gift of myrrh represents healing.

(Were they really kings? Their gifts seen to represent kingship. But whose? I choose to believe that the kingly gifts of gold, frankincense and myrrh relate to the Kingship of the baby born at Christmas.)

And do read T.S. Eliot's lovely poem, 'The Journey of the Magi'.

A birthday cake for Jesus

Pick some free evening (the nearer to Christmas the better), ideally on Christmas Day, to have a birthday party for Jesus. (A cake can be baked ahead and frozen to avoid making the day *too* busy.)

Let children decorate the cake to say 'Happy Birthday, Jesus'. Place a candle for each family member. Each person should light one candle and wish Jesus a Happy Birthday. Then jointly sing 'Happy Birthday' to Him.

Then eat with lots of laughter, ice cream and party decorations (if available).

You might even want to choose a project for your family or an offering for your church to give to symbolise a gift to Jesus for His birthday. ('If you have done it to one of the least of these, you've done it unto me' – Matthew 25:40.)

A snack for Santa

As I was growing up, we had a custom of leaving a snack by the fireplace for Father Christmas. On Christmas morning, the very first thing I did was run to see if he had eaten my snack. To my delight, he always had.

I'm not sure why I enjoyed this custom so, but I still do – as I've carried on the meaningless-but-fun tradition with my girls.

Elizabeth, five, this year gave me this incredulous look for forgetting a drink for Santa. 'But Mummy,' she said, 'what if he's thirsty too?' Amazing how thoughtful five-year-olds can be!

(I do not put great stress on Santa Claus, for I do not want to overstress Santa to the exclusion of Jesus. However, I see no point in spoiling a legend for children, who will find out soon enough the harsh realities of life.)

DID YOU KNOW . . .
that in many European countries Santa comes on the evening of 5 December? They call him St Nicholas – who was a bishop in Asia Minor in the fourth century. He was a man of great compassion, and word of his generosity spread far and wide. He used to leave gifts secretly for those in need – hence the tradition of his coming secretly (on a white horse) and leaving gifts for children.

The mythical 'spirit of giving' goes by many different names:

Denmark – *Julmanden* – carried by reindeer
Sweden – *Yul Tomten* – an elf
Italy – *La Befana* – an old woman with gifts
Switzerland – *Mother Christmas* goes with *Father Christmas*

Making Birthdays Special

How do you make birthdays special for family members? Mainly by thoughtfulness and sensitivity to that person's special loves. Try:

1 breakfast in bed
2 special (inexpensive) surprises made by each family member
3 his favourite menu for tea
4 a bit of money to spend any way he likes
5 an addition to his favourite hobby or collection
6 a family outing of his own choosing
7 a poem (or song) written about him
8 fresh flowers in his room
9 fresh sheets on his bed
10 the day off from his regular chores
11 a poster created by other family members especially for him
12 a cake shaped in his latest fancy

13 a long-distance phone call to anyone he chooses
14 a book or record token

Making Sundays Special

How many ways can you make Sunday special? As many as your creativity dreams up!

Here are my favourites:

1 Make Sunday dinner a special meal. Plan your menu ahead (even before Saturday). Make your pudding on Saturday. Do as much of the preparation as possible on Saturday, so Sunday morning won't be too rushed for relaxation.
2 Use your best china, flowers, candles, or anything else that says 'special' to your family.
3 Devote certain menus to be eaten only on Sundays (roast lamb, or lasagne).
4 Stay dressed up in Sunday clothes until after dinner. (Yes, you'll have to eat neatly.)
5 Plan to have a brief worship time after the meal.
6 Keep Sundays family or invite company to relax with you but *don't* clean the house, go shopping or keep weekday routines. After all, God did intend Sunday as a day to enjoy and rest. Don't you *want* a day off? I do.
7 Take a walk together.
8 Reserve certain games to play together only on Sundays.

Party cakes to amaze even yourself!

Party cakes needn't be daunting. Even I (of little patience) have managed Hallowe'en cats and (my latest birthday feat) a pink castle.

For some really amazingly simple shapes try the ideas in the *Busy Mum's Baking Cookbook* by Wendy Craig (Hamlyn, 1985):

traffic lights	dominoes	dice
cricket bats	butterflies	trains
roller skates	clowns	prams
pencil boxes	horses	

She gives you the blow-by-blow baking instructions and I think even I could follow them.

If you're really energetic, you can even make a gingerbread house. Bake your basic gingerbread dough fairly thick (½ inch), so it won't crack. (See the gingerbead men reciple in Chapter 8.) You'll need six flat panels for walls and pitched roof. (You determine the size of the house yourself.)

'Glue' the walls together with very thick icing. Decorating is the fun (and easiest) part. Use gumdrops, rope liquorice, raisins, marshmallows, virtually any sweet, and pipe on windows, etc. with more of your gooey icing.

Have fun! And remember, even if it flops, it'll taste good and the memory of the making will last forever in your children's minds (and hearts).

4 A simple lifestyle

'Simplify, simplify'

Henry David Thoreau

Simple living isn't just an alternate lifestyle. It's a biblical command. Did you realise that Jesus spoke more often of the 'poor' than of heaven? There must be a good reason.

Matthew 25 confronts us with others in need of food, drink, clothing, warmth and comfort (in prison and in sickness). To whom were these commands to care for them addressed? ·To the followers of Jesus – US!

If we use all our income on ourselves, we'll have nothing left to give the poor. But do we actually need to use ALL our income? Probably not. There are endless ways to economise, to save – *so that we can give away* the extra.

I know what you're thinking: 'Easy for you to say, but you don't know MY budget'. Oh, but I do. We've had virtually no income (during the writing of this book) since we decided my husband would quit his job to research for his PhD. We've learned to live on far less and even to like it this way.

So the ideas contained in this chapter, which began of necessity, now seem to me the only way to live. All of the suggestions may not suit your style, but could you change your style? If not, at least adopt some simple lifestyle habits – if only because your kids would rather make things than buy them.

Simple living becomes its own reward in that what you *don't own* doesn't require cleaning, storing or insuring. We now live with no phone, no car and no electrical appliances other than a hair dryer – and I LIKE IT! No one calls interrupting family devotions, the car never breaks down and I don't even miss what I don't have. Life is too short (and too valuable) to spend worrying over 'things'. The less you own, the freer your time – and money.

And if you have any doubts left, remember the goats at the end of Matthew 25!

The fundamental approach to simple living is: make your own. So most of the following are ideas for doing just that.

Mañana

The Latin Americans have a saying, '*mañana*', which means 'tomorrow'. Or, more accurately, it means 'the tomorrow which never comes'.

Strange as it sounds, one way of implementing a simple lifestyle is to put things off as long as you can – without buying, that is. *Whatever* it is you need to replace, wait one more day or one more week.

I often practise this with grocery shopping by taking it as a challenge to see what I have in the kitchen that I can make a meal of *without having to go to the store for one more day*. It's amazing what you can do with a bit of bread, a few eggs, a few vegetables. Invent a delightful new quiche. Or leftovers make nourishing soups.

Or try this technique with buying clothes: A few months ago I wanted a certain pair of shoes. I earmarked some money I knew I would receive from a speaking engagement to buy them.

However, the day after I received the money (a Sunday) we had a missions speaker at church challenging us to forgo some expenditure that wasn't essential, and to give the money to missions. He used as illustration giving one shirt if you had two. Well, I had more than one pair of shoes. So how else could I respond?

So I asked God to help me make better use of the shoes I had and I still haven't bought any more. We *can* get along with less if we are willing.

The same principle applies to buying an appliance or a car. Use them until they die a natural death. Don't buy anything because yours isn't the latest model. You'll be amazed at how much money this habit saves.

Ten ways to live a more peaceful family existence

Yes, Heaven is everywhere at home,
The big, blue cap that always fits.

G.K. Chesterton,
The Napoleon of Notting Hill

You've no doubt visited homes where everything seemed to run smoothly and no one appeared ruffled or hurried. And you dreamed that you could live that way. You can. It takes some arranging but it's well worth it!

1 Keep noise levels to a minimum. Turn off the TV and radio while eating meals. Don't run the washer while eating if it's near the dining room (as ours is). Turn off any noise that can be dispensed with at all times of the day. Silence produces peace.

2 Write out an assignment list for chores each day. This should avoid

squabbles over whose turn it is to take out the rubbish or wash dishes.

3 Don't over-extend yourselves individually or as a family. Be realistic in how many evenings a week you or your children can go out and still remain stress-free. The normal routines of life do take up most of our time. Dropping one activity could free a lot of leisure time. (Even as I write this, I am trying to decide which activity I could give up and feel less pressured.)

4 Assess household routines and determine if some of them are unnecessary. Are your standards of cleanliness creating bondage for you? Simplify any work that must be done and set yourself free from neurotic tendencies like washing on Mondays, ironing towels or eating precisely at 5.45. You will feel more relaxed and so all the family will benefit.

5 Remember things. Write notes, use a bulletin board in the kitchen, keep a daily diary with a 'To Do' list, or whatever system works best for you. But life will run more smoothly for everyone if time is not wasted in the frustration of looking for lost objects. (They're NEVER lost at a convenient time.)

6 Add pleasure into routine whenever possible. Play music loud enough for everyone in the house to hear as they tackle various household chores in various rooms. Take a hug break. Plan a story reading session when a certain job is done.

7 Combine efforts to tackle a job that would overtax one family member and thus bring stress on all. I often ask my family at supper to give me half an hour to put the flat to rights again. If I've been too busy writing to clean the house, everyone pitches in for half an hour and saves me an evening of displeasure and frustration (at their sitting while I am still working).

8 Add any beauty you can to the atmosphere of your home. Plants freshen the air and definitely freshen my spirits. I love a cyclamen I was given because it blooms continually. All I have to do is stop and stare at its loveliness to restore me to equanimity.

Beauty, for you, might be art, lovely furnishings or uncluttered space. Beauty also produces peace and feelings of well-being. (It also says to your children that they are important enough for you to plan your home for their pleasure.)

9 Keep the house as clutter-free as possible. Cluttered surroundings clutter our spirits as well. Put away unused objects or furniture. Keep the floor spaces free and make sure everyone knows where everything in the house belongs.

10 Give undivided attention to your children *when they ask*. I realise there are times when you can't drop what you're doing (i.e. drop the baby to listen to the toddler). But it's far less stressful on all involved if you can quickly meet the need of an insistent two (or four or fourteen)-year-old than to put them off and listen to their continued begging. Stop what you are doing. Look them in the eye. Meet the

need and then you can all dwell in harmony together.

Clothes swap

If you're like me, you have clothes in your wardrobe that you're either tired of, are not the right size for or which are simply lost in a crowded closet.

What to do with these clothes that are still good but just not 'you' any more?

Organise a clothes swap in your neighbourhood or church. You can swap, barter or sell but don't let them sit unused. Recently a friend and I (about the same size) swapped a lot of things and both of us gained new clothes without spending a penny!

Why not organise a children's swap while you're at it? Children's clothes are outgrown before they wear out. Find a child in your church who is one step down from yours and pass them on. (I am assuming no one would pass on torn, stained or otherwise ruined items.)

Whatever is left, box up and mail to whatever missionary your church supports.They will gladly take your leftovers. Everyone could make a small donation to the postage (from the savings on the clothing swap).

Apple dumplings night

For a delicious, meatless meal, we've adopted a tradition from my husband's family. As a minister's family with seven children, they quickly learned shortcuts for feeding that hungry brood. Thus, 'apple dumplings for supper' became not just a tradition, but a treat. For when you have 'apple dumplings for supper', apple dumplings are ALL you have for supper. Now before you dismiss the idea of having only pudding for supper, read the recipe. It has wholemeal flour in the dumplings and far more apples than sugar. (See next page.)

A non-spending week?

'A non-spending week – you've got to be kidding, thinking this.' But it IS possible. Here's how:

Several years ago, I read this simple lifestyle idea and was as shocked as you. But we found ourselves with more month than money and decided to try it.

What you do is prepare ahead by:

1 Filling the car with petrol.
2 Buying a week's supply of food. (Yes, you CAN.)
3 Anything else can wait.
4 Anything you run out of – substitute or do without.

It's that simple. But I think you'll find that the real problem is not what you MUST have. Rather, you are hooked on *buying*. You don't *need*, but you *want*.

So what you are really doing is disciplining yourself not to buy non-essentials. Obviously, you may need more petrol or a trip to the dentist. But

Dumplings

For six large apples. You may find, as I have, that six just isn't enough. If so, double the recipe – it's still cheap!

4 oz. wholemeal flour	4 oz. vegetable shortening
4 oz. plain flour	4 teaspoons baking
½ teaspoon salt	powder
½ teaspoon cream of	⅓ pt. milk
tartar	2 tablespoons sugar

Mix all this together and add enough flour to enable you to roll it out. Cut into 6 squares.

Spicy 'soup' (to bake them in)

Set oven to gas mark 6, 400°F

1 pint water	6 cooking apples
1 tablespoon cinnamon	4 oz. raisins
1 tablespoon nutmeg	6 oz. sugar
1 tablespoon mixed spice	Cinnamon and brown
	sugar to taste

Add spices and sugar to water, bring to a boil and have ready to pour over dumplings. Core apples and place in centre of dough squares. Fill well with raisins, cinnamon and a pinch of brown sugar (if you like them sweet). Wrap dough squares up around apples to cover them completely. Place in a deep baking dish, pour spicy 'soup' over them,, and bake for about 45 minutes.

Phil would add that apple dumplings aren't complete until you pour milk over them.

you can save a *lot* of money by not spending that 'extra' you don't have.

After you've succeeded with one week, try two or three – or three months, as the book I read suggested.

What you do with the extra is up to you, but the experiment in discipline is worth trying.

More simple lifestyle ideas

Jumble Sales

Do *nice* people go to jumble sales? Yes, if they're sensible.

We bought Elizabeth's winter coat for 25p (grey wool with hood and not even a lost button). Phil found a never-worn pair of trainers his size for 10p.

I could bore you with an interminable list but you get the idea. Second-hand shops and jumble sales haven't much aesthetic appeal, but beauty I can find elsewhere.

Furthermore, 'new' needn't be your cardinal rule in buying. Why must we have everything *new*? If it's in good condition and good quality, why does 'new' enter the question? Obviously, you must look things over carefully, but then I've bought things new that were damaged or of inferior quality.

Walking versus Riding

DON'T get in the car unless you intend to go at least a mile (or you plan to buy a 50 lb. bag of potatoes). Walk.

Most of us need more exercise than we get. Doctors decided long ago that walking is the best exercise. If your only walk is around the block with the dog, you need more aerobic stimulation.

Walking also forces us to slow down and enjoy life. It takes a bit longer, but you can plan menus, sing or pray on the way.

Children love walking. They stop to look at insects, birds, most everything, making it an educational jaunt.

You'll obviously save money on petrol and probably even lose some weight! What a bargain!

Vegetarian food

I can hear the groans now. But we've been eating almost totally vegetarian for several months and my family is not complaining. The trick is to cook high-protein food and plenty of it. (You can afford to cook plenty because of the savings on meat.) Have a look at some vegetarian cookbooks before you rule it out. No, we don't eat seaweed – we haven't gone that far: but we are all feeling better and even losing weight.

Begin by eating a meatless meal one day a week. Experiment with various rice or pasta and vegetable combinations. Add cheese and they'll think it's great!

Cigarettes and alcohol

I read recently that the average household spends seven per cent of its weekly income on cigarettes and alcohol. I was staggered!

Neither contribute to nutrition or health. In fact, both are harmful to health.

Try a fast from cigarettes and alcohol and see how much further your budget stretches.

Or take it a bit more seriously, and donate that income to world hunger. You can save lives with the savings from these non-essentials.

Freezer Soup

A woman can make a meal of random spoons of leftovers

Old Kathy's saying

One really easy meal to save for a busy day is what I call 'freezer soup'.

You simply save every spoonful of leftover veggies, broth, macaroni, etc. Dump these bits into a plastic container you keep in the freezer. When the container is full, pull it out on a busy day and put in the slo-cooker while you go about your busy-ness. (A slo-cooker pays for itself in no time. It takes very little electricity since the heat remains low. And it saves worlds of time on busy days.)

Not only is this a virtually free meal (because you might have thrown out all the spoonsful), but it couldn't be quicker! That's what I call simple living!

Any day I know fixing a nutritious supper will be a race against time, I put supper in the slo-cooker and, like magic, it's ready when I am. You can cook stews, meats, vegetables or casseroles – even sweets – in a slo-cooker. You put them on early in the day and leave them simmering quietly all day. (They're great for working Mums especially.)

Some of our favourite slo-cooker meals are

spaghetti layered several times with sauce and cheese (see Chapter 5 for recipe)
apples and granola cooked overnight and ready for breakfast
chicken, potato and carrot hotpot
chili
scalloped potatoes
steamed puddings
cabbage, carrots, potatoes and German sausage chunks.

Make your own greeting cards

Handmade cards are far more interesting than bought ones. Children come up with such imaginative ideas. (The card companies should employ children!)

Keep a supply of coloured sugar paper and good markers (such as Coloursticks by Berol) and turn over the family greeting business to your kids. Give them orders well in advance and let them produce birthday, Easter and Christmas cards. And don't forget Valentines. (A few lace doilies and a gold pen produce superb Valentines.)

Experiment with different artistic effects such as tracing, stencilling, potato printing, watercolour and/or acrylic painting, pressed flowers under clear film, calligraphy, and embroidery or tapestry on card.

Handmade cards needn't be second class. Your children might even perfect some variety and sell them to friends.

Co-ops

By a 'co-op', I mean a group of people who go together to buy food in bulk and then share it.

Buying in large volume is loads cheaper. And all we can save, means more to give to the Third World, where food is not plentiful or cheap.

Start small. Buy a 55 lb. bag of potatoes and share it with another family. If you think it's not worth the effort, let me share a few figures.

We were paying 18p per pound for potatoes in the autumn. However, a 55 lb. bag cost £2.50. Fifty-five times 18p is £9.90. We saved £7.40 on just one bag of potatoes.

We stored it in a cold shed and our neighbours saw it and decided to do the same. So the two families saved a nice little bit for the world's economy. You think seven pounds doesn't matter in the world's economy? What if everyone bought in volume and shared?

Another larger scale co-op involves buying flour, sugar, oats, nuts, dried fruits, rice, etc., in large volume and selling it by the pound.

Mention it to your friends. Gather those interested for an organisational meeting. Decide on a storage place and then formulate an order.

From there, you can sell by the pound to this group only or to outsiders. All you really need is scales for weighing and plastic bags.

A group of Christians could take it on as a money-making project and send the savings to a world hunger organisation. Why not?

Useful books

Book of Practical Household Formulas Thorsons publishers, 1975.
Home Grown Food, **Roy Genders**, Michael Joseph, 1976.
Rich Christians in an Age of Hunger, **Ron Sider**, Hodder and Stoughton, 1978.

5 Entertaining

'Share with God's people, who are in need. Practise hospitality.'

Romans 12:13

Entertaining is my favourite biblical command. I like people. I like to cook. Thus, it's easy for me to invite people to our house to share food and fellowship. It was only natural that I should include a chapter on entertaining as a family.

Probably because Phil and I enjoy entertaining, our children have caught the joy as well. They never know who or how many or what nationality of people they'll find at our table – and they love it. (See the section on Christmas in Chapter 3.)

However, entertaining does take time and effort. You MUST either like it, or see it as a biblical command to be obeyed – joyfully. (Don't entertain grudgingly. Your guests will sense it immediately.)

Entertaining is a good lesson in servanthood. Jesus didn't have a home from which to entertain others. But he salvaged a wedding feast by making wine, and washed the feet of his disciples (the servant's job).

Entertaining can also be a ministry. Some of the best examples of Grace have come to me at a low point in my life while *being entertained* in someone's home. Those showers of grace refreshed my soul and I vowed that I would do that for others someday. Maybe you'd like to begin such a ministry . . .

The real reason for entertaining

Perhaps I should say a word about my philosophy of entertaining.

I view it as a ministry. Everybody needs a break from routine (or cooking) and everybody needs to feel appreciated by others. By inviting others to my home and serving them, I am offering both affirmation and relaxation to them. They are wanted in my home and I do my best to make them comfortable.

So I MUST NOT MAKE THEM UNCOMFORTABLE BY TRYING TO IMPRESS THEM. People can tell whether you are entertaining to impress, or simply because you desire their company.

You cannot entertain for ministry and entertain to impress at the same time. Karen Burton Mains addresses this topic well in her book *Open Heart, Open Home* (published in the USA by David C. Cook, 1975). I recommend it highly to anyone who has ever given thought to entertaining as a ministry.

But even if you don't consider your entertaining a ministry, simplicity and a desire to serve, rather than to impress, will go farther towards putting your guests at ease.

I cannot emphasise simplicity enough. My main rule is cheap food, but plenty of it. Served with love, you can't miss.

Check your motives. Pray over whom you entertain and how. Make your entertaining a ministry of love to someone who needs a bit of pampering.

Read again who Jesus would have us entertain in Luke 14:16-24.

Free ways to offer hospitality
(and God's love)

Hospitality needn't take time and a lot of money. All it requires is a bit of thoughtfulness. Try some of these relatively painless ways of including others into your plans.

1 Offer a ride to a neighbour when you pick up children at school, run to a grocery, etc.
2 Likewise, invite newcomers to do all of the above, and to go to more interesting places as well.
3 Offer hot chocolate to the neighbourhood kids – and their mums, when convenient.
4 Give someone a certificate for specific tasks you will perform for them (i.e. babysitting for a young mum, typing for the student, errands for an elderly person).

5 When you sit down to take a break, call a new neighbour for an impromptu cuppa.
6 Plan a sewing evening with another woman you've been meaning to get to know. You can talk and mend clothing at the same time.
7 Plan an impromptu supper with some other family. Call them up and ask what they're having and put it all together no matter what the menus. The kids won't care and you can enjoy the fellowship with no real effort entailed.

Children can help with entertaining

'All I want is for them to stay out of my way while I get ready for company.' Have you ever thought that? I have. But children want (and need) to be included in family events. And there are lots of details they can take care of for you.

Young children (3+) can

pick flowers for the table
choose or arrange seating
draw creative placecards for guests
set the table
crack and beat eggs
butter the bread
serve appetizers
greet guests
knead dough

Older children (6+) can

create centrepieces
help elderly guest to the table
assemble hors d'oeuvres
clear dishes afterwards (or wash up
dishes from preparation)
look after younger children or
guests' children
hang up coats
anything on the younger children's list
cook some things with simple recipes

They just might be of more help than
you thought!

Ready anytime!

Most hostesses need all the time-savers
possible. Because you never know
when company will arrive, or when
your schedule will go awry despite
careful planning, keep goodies on hand
for emergencies:

1 A sponge baked and frozen (but not
iced) for trifle or to be iced.
2 A packet of special biscuits hidden for
that special friend who drops in for tea.
3 A good-sized casserole, frozen and
ready for unexpected guests.
4 Fruity breads baked and frozen. Or,
if you don't have a large freezer, a box
of fruit bread mix.
5 An extra tin of coffee and a box of
juice (for children), as well as boxed
UHT milk and hot cocoa mix (there's a
recipe for this in Chapter 8).
6 In the cupboard, keep coconut,
almonds, stuffing mix, tinned

mushrooms, cream of mushroom soup
and a large assortment of spices to jazz
up an ordinary meal if company drops
in.
7 Extra stores of rice, pasta and lentils
can quickly be turned into soup or
casserole with whatever else you have
on hand.

Sometimes we must choose between
saving money and saving time. Nearly
always, homemade food is cheaper
than ready-made, and it's usually more
nutritious and tastier too! To make my
homemade meals the least time-
consuming, I make a lot of my dishes
(especially baked goods), from scratch,
in bulk, and freeze half for the future.
Then I'm ready any time – well, almost.

Atmosphere makes all the difference

Atmosphere can make or break a
gathering and a little planning can
make all the difference.

1 Create a glow of warmth with soft
lights, candles, a fire in the fireplace,
and pleasant background music.
2 Houseplants add an aura of comfort
and airiness to a room. For the
evening, gather and arrange them in
your lounge or dining room.
3 Pine cones and baskets add to a
room's texture and interest.
4 Plan topics for discussion if you
anticipate conversational problems.
5 You might want to include a short

devotional after you eat (depending on the group).

6 Don't forget the influence of the sense of smell. Boil spicy aromatics just before guests arrive. Simmer (uncovered) sixteen whole cloves, 3 sticks of cinnamon and one tablespoon of mixed spice in a quart of water. Store in a jar in the fridge for later use.

Centrepieces and decorations for entertaining

If you're anything like I am, you don't think of yourself as particularly creative. My old standby centrepiece is whichever of my violets happens to be in bloom. However, with a little time and even less money, anyone can turn out some stunning centrepieces.

A single flower blossom (rose, chrysanthemum, iris, peony) floating on water in a cut glass bowl.
Several candles of differing heights with fabric ribbon tied in a bow around each.
A wreath of flowers or greenery (artificial, if you must), filled with fruit.
A variety of clear glass bottles filled with coloured water. Light candles near them to make your own rainbow.
A pumpkin filled with soup or a melon

filled with fruit salad. Think in terms of incorporating the centrepiece into the menu. As an extra touch, give your centrepiece to the first one to compliment you on it.

You can add homemade elegance by making your own tablecloths and napkins to match. Then bring out your best dishes and handmade, even childmade, place cards. Fringe gingham squares to make napkins with a country charm. Think creatively. Amost anything of beauty can be used.

Theme evenings: putting it all together

Just for the fun of it, I concocted several complete entertaining extravanganzas. Here's your theme, menu and decorations. What are you waiting for?

European elegance

Atmosphere: romantic and simple.
Decor: checked tablecloths on small tables, simple vases of fresh flowers.
Size group: small and intimate.
Menu: several varieties of cheese, hard breads (unsliced loaves), a good soup or quiche, fresh fruis with cream cheese dips, sparkling apple and grape juice.
Music: Tchaikovsky.

German Oktoberfest

Atmosphere: lighthearted, joyful and homey.

Decor: as colourful as possible, blooming houseplants.
Size group: adaptable.
Menu: Knackwurst or bratwurst on pumpernickel rolls, sauerkraut, German potato salad and strudels.
Music: upbeat brass band sound (if you can't find recordings of yodellers in your local library).

Mexican Fiesta

Atmosphere: celebration
Decor: straw hat centrepiece, hanging **pinata** (see below), lots of red and black.
Size of group: adaptable.
Menu: taco salad, enchiladas, nacho chips, apple burritos, spicy punch. (Look for a Mexican cookery book at the library.)
Music: Mexican tap-dancing variety.
A **pinata** is a bag of some sort full of sweets. Mexicans do it up in papier mâché. You blindfold children or guests and give them a stick to swing at the hanging bag, to try to break it open and share the sweets.

Hawaiian Luau

Atmosphere: lazy and warm.
Decor: large houseplants grouped near food table, bright pinks, blues and greens, at least one fresh pineapple for decoration as well as flower leis (artificial if you must) to wear.
Size group: large.
Menu: ham glazed in pineapple sauce, whole baked apples (unpeeled, just cored), green salad and fruit salad served in coconut halves.
Music: Hawaiian stringed melodies.

My favourite entertaining standbys

Do not forget to entertain strangers, for by so doing some people have entertained angels without knowing it.

Hebrews 13:2

I have several menus that come to mind when I think 'company'. They are all easy and economical and definite crowd pleasers.

1 Stir-fried veggies and rice (serves 6-8)
This is composed of whatever vegetables I have on hand but usually includes (chopped)

onions, peppers, carrots, garlic, tomatoes
broccoli or cauliflower
green peas or green beans
and sometimes beef, chicken or pork chunks

This is stir-fried in a wok with one tablespoon of oil. Simultaneously, steam one pound of rice.

Season with curry powder and salt. Or you can make it sweet and sour by combining equal amounts of oil and cider vinegar, a tablespoon of brown sugar and a bit of ketchup.

Then I usually mix it all together and serve it from the wok to look more oriental.

There's any number of variations, depending on what you have on hand. This has become Angela's favourite meal, despite the fact that we rarely use meat unless we have company.

2   Lasagne is Phil's favourite. Again I often omit mince and substitute chopped frozen spinach and mushrooms in the basic recipe. And it makes lots for a crowd, though not as cheaply as stir-fried rice.

3   Slo-cooker spaghetti is a good Sunday dinner menu because it won't burn and is ready as soon as you're home from church. Cook spaghetti and layer with a spicy spaghetti sauce and grated Cheddar cheese (or Mozzarella or Parmesan). Layer twice or three times and pour ¼ pint of water into the bottom to keep it from sticking. Leave in slo-cooker three hours on high. A lovely blending of flavours – don't forget the oregano. (You can add a layer of cooked mince if you like.)

Slo-cookers are worth their weight in gold. They use very little electricity and save overwhelming amounts of time and hassle. Just put the food in, go away and come back to find supper all cooked. Great for working mums!

4   Beef stew is great for cold winter nights. I make this in the slo-cooker as well, saving hassles of last-minute preparation. Just toast some garlic bread and add a salad.

Beef stew consists of chunks of browned beef, chunks of parboiled carrots, potatoes and onion. The flavour is enhanced by sage and lots of black pepper.

5   Club-sandwiches are an American favourite that we enjoy for casual entertaining.

Just buy as many Vienna loaves as you reckon for your crowd. Buy spicy cold meats like corned beef or your family favourties. Cut the loaves lengthwise and layer with cold meats, cheese slices, tomato slices, onion slices and shredded lettuce. The crowning glory of a club is a mixture of oil and vinegar and spice sprinkled on. Then put the top halves on and slice through into great, fat chunks of sandwiches. Add potato salad and raw veggies for an American feast.

6 **Chicken, broccoli and rice** is another of Angela's favourites (and mine).

Combine large pieces of cooked chicken with stems of cooked broccoli and rice (which has butter and cheese melted into it). Pour over this a can of evaporated milk and bake an hour in the oven. Yummy.

Zany entertaining

For informal evenings of fun, try one of these ideas:

1 For a large group of couples, have each couple bring a **boxed dinner for two**. Upon arrival, take them from guests and then draw numbers to choose a boxed dinner. You provide drinks and dessert. Or ask guests to bring dessert only and swap as above.

2 Ask guest to bring a piece or two of various fruits: bananas, oranges, a tin of crushed pineapple, nuts, candied cherries, coconut or kiwi. You prepare two pizza crusts and cover with a layer of sweetened cream cheese. Then everyone helps create decorative **fruit pizzas** with the fruit they brought. Bake as you would pizzas and devour! (This can be done similarly with regular pizza toppings.)

3 Host a **biscuit-painting party!** Mix up your favourite dough for cut-out biscuits (usually the dough you refrigerate first, works best). Chill and have ready to roll out. Let guests cut their own biscuits and paint them with a beaten egg yolk mixed with a few drops of food colouring. Prepare several colours ready to brush on with paint brushes. Bake them and judge the most artistic.

4 **Mystery dinners** are great for an easy-going group. You plan and cook a meal for the entire group. Then create a menu to give guests, on which the real menu is coded. You can use names of cities, or people or whatever you like. Include in the list on the menu the cutlery, water, napkin, butter, etc. Then each person chooses three coded items and must finish that course before going on to the next. (If he chooses three food items with no cutlery, he must eat without it until he accidentally chooses it from his menu.) We did this with some student friends and laughed hysterically as Mark drank his peas from his glass – since he had no cutlery.

5 **A progressive dinner** requires co-operation with several hostesses. You eat the soup course at one home, then move to another home for the main course, another for dessert and another

for tea and sweets. A nice event for couples for a special evening out. (A bit more difficult with children.)

6 Or plan a meal of **hot hors-d'oeuvres**. Invite as many people as you like and ask each to bring her favourite hot hors-d'oeuvre (sweet and sour meatballs, individual quiches, etc.) It makes an unusual menu, but one that everyone loves.

Javanese dinner: easy menu for a big crowd

The first time I ate this particular menu was at a missionary convention where over 100 people were eating lunch. The ladies at the host church had set up this missionary menu lunch and, strange as it was to us, *it was delicious!*

The best thing about the Javanese dinner is that so much of it can be prepared ahead – even days before. So the next time you're entertaining a crowd, do it Javanese style.

Another good feature is that you can add or delete according to taste and no one will ever think anything is missing.

Main components:
cooked rice
curried chicken (shredded) in plenteous broth

Serve buffet style and let everyone 'build their own'.

Toppings:

almonds	shredded lettuce
chopped onions	grated cheese
raisins	coconut
celery chunks	crushed pineapple
tomato wedges	chow mein noodles

It may sound too mixed up, but leave it to your guests to decide how mixed up they like it.

For dessert: fruit salad, of course.

This menu is healthy, relatively inexpensive and delicious!

Simple entertaining ideas

1 Popcorn and **Trivial Pursuit**.
2 Make-a-pizza night (guests bring various ingredients).
3 A hot potato party – consisting of baked potatoes and a variety of toppings.
4 Hot hors-d'oeuvres and literary readings.
5 Talent night and ice cream sundaes.
6 A sixties evening – include dress, music and some food fad from the sixties.
7 A dieter's support group – salads and diet tip-sharing.
8 Rice and water fund-raiser for world hunger.
9 Biscuit exchange to help out with Christmas baking pressures.
10 A recipe party – where everyone brings their favourite recipes and a sample of one to taste.
11 Hot dog roasts over the fireplace and games with another family.
12 Potluck soup for a cold winter's evening. Guests bring a surprise soup ingredient and it evolves as you go. Watch a video together while it simmers.
13 Progressive dinners – moving to a different home for each course. Dress up and make it a romantic evening out.

6 Family projects you can live to tell about

The words 'Family Project' may scare you off with visions of colossal messes and great expense.

On the contrary, family projects may be as simple as planning a party for an OAP friend or a day of gardening together.

The only requirement for family projects is togetherness.

Family, by definition, means a joint effort. It may be joint effort in preparing for Christmas, or it may be cleaning the cellar. Whichever is the case, concentrate on enjoying togetherness.

When I say to Elizabeth (my five-year-old), 'Let's do a project', her face lights up. 'What project?' she asks excitedly. For 'project' to Elizabeth means a creative activity done with Mummy – and there's nothing she likes better. (This definition evolved because creating is her passion in life.)

But if 'project' doesn't denote fun to you, seek to approach jobs that must be done with the positive attitude of creativity. Enthusiasm is highly contagious and your positive attitude can transform a day of gardening into a party.

Fun projects (like decorating the house for Christmas) need little encouragement. But concentrating on the joy of togetherness can save a day of drudgery and complaints.

Most of the family projects in this chapter are for fun, but you can apply these same three principles to fun and work alike.

1 Attitude determines atmosphere.
2 A few little treats transform anything into a party.
3 Rewards for goals accomplished heighten motivation.

So set out with enthusiasm. Plan a refreshment break. Most importantly, offer a reward for a project well done.

(Note: when I say 'reward', I am thinking of favourite biscuits or a promised trip to the zoo, not money.)

Goals for family projects

You can make a family project of absolutely any interest. Simply think it out a bit to adapt it to all family members and then *enthusiastically* sell them on it.

1 **Educational goals?** Make a game of family research on birds, ancient Egypt or your family tree. See who can find out the most and then compile all the info into a notebook or album.
2 **Art?** Take a drawing course as a family at your local college. My

daughter, Angela, and I attended a pottery course. She was the only child enrolled but she learned to 'throw' clay as well as the rest. In gaining a skill, she also gained in her self-image – feeling herself to be a talented person.

3 Missions? Again, there are as many ways as your imagination can conjure. For specific ideas, see Chapter 10.

4 Hobbies? Choose a hobby everyone's interested in and go with it. Put in as much money and time as you can squeeze into it, for what you're really doing is investing time and love in each other.

Crafts for fun and profit

Choose a craft that all the family can get excited about. You might even want to mass produce and sell some, to fund a family outing or missions project. Try

1 candlemaking
2 ice sculpture
3 stencilling (walls or small items for gifts – see below)
4 speciality cooking (crêpes, confections or exotic cuisine)
5 spinning and weaving (from raw wool)
6 copper engraving
7 leathercrafting
8 woodworking
9 machine knitting
10 speciality photography (such as nature, for example)
11 printing (with a press)
12 making jewellery
13 calligraphy
14 pottery
15 macrame
16 painting
17 doll making
18 speciality gardening (to sell flowers or vegetables)

Candlemaking

This is really very simple. To make a basic, solid colour candle, follow the instructions below.

1 Use old candle ends or wax (paraffin) bought in a hardware store.
2 Place a large, clean tin in a pan of hot water. Keep the heat low and melt the wax slowly. (It won't catch fire as long as it is kept at low heat.)
3 Colour with broken crayon bits to desired shade.
4 If using old candle ends, fish out the leftover wicks.
5 Use any heavy string for wicking. But dip it in wax and lay aside before pouring candle.
6 Use any container to mould candles, but lightly grease first. (Unless you mean to leave candle in glass container, etc.)
7 Melt wax only long enough to become liquid. Don't leave a long time on heat after it reaches liquid stage.
8 Set your chosen mould on a newspaper (in case of spills).
9 Attach wick through bottom of container if you're using a milk carton. If bottom of container is solid, position

one end of wick in centre of container. The other end, tie around a table knife and balance knife across top of container to keep it centred.
10 Pour melted wax into container slowly and carefully. Adjust knife so wick falls down through centre of container.
11 Leave several hours without moving.
12 Carefully remove candle from mould. Trim wick and enjoy!

Stencilling

This is simple but exacting.

1 Buy a sheet of clear, flexible plastic.
2 Choose a design and trace onto a sheet of white paper.
3 Using a craft knife, cut design out of plastic (which is laid over design).
4 Now that you have your stencil cut, decide what you want to decorate. Stencilling looks great as a border on walls, or on pillows, on small wooden items or just to frame.
5 Place the stencil where you desire and tape into place (at corners).
6 Use a small sponge, dipped in paint, but not dripping. Paint can be oil or acrylic but not watercolour.
7 Press sponge firmly over stencil. Brush lightly to make sure your corners and detail appear.
8 Ideally, leave stencil attached to object to dry. But if you need to remove to use again immediately, you must be very careful in lifting it or it will smear.

9 Allow stencilled item to dry overnight untouched.

Adopt a granny

Is there an older person in your neighbourhood or church who lives alone? Make attempts to get to know her and potentially adopt her into your family. How to begin?

Drop in to visit this person and introduce yourself or get further acquainted. (Go without the children on your first visit.)
Invite her to family tea some evening to meet the rest of the family.
Bake biscuits and send one of the children to deliver them and visit her.
Include her in family holiday celebrations if she has no family nearby.
Offer to mow her grass or do odd jobs for her.
Ask her to babysit after you have established a solid friendship.
Take her with you to run errands when she needs a ride.
Have the children include her on their handmade Christmas card and Valentine lists.
Give her a subscription to a magazine she would enjoy.

After you are well acquainted, instinct will take over. You won't need my suggestions any more. And everyone will benefit from the friendship.

A foster child for us?

The child that is not clean and neat
With lots of toys and things to eat
He is a naughty child, I'm sure —
Or else his dear papa is poor.

Robert Louis Stevenson,
Looking Forward

Melda Mendoza, 12, lives in the Philippines, one of ten children in her family. Her father cannot earn enough to feed them all and life is hard for them.

How do I know her? She was the child we sponsored through Holy Land Christian Mission International, an organisation attempting to balance the world's wealth (moving it from west to east).

Jesus talked a lot about widows, orphans and the poor. Old Testament Jewish society had laws to ensure their protection and no one starved.

Not so these days. The world's wealth is crazily and unfairly distributed. And we, as Christians, must attempt to right this wrong. One of the ways we can help the poor is by sponsoring orphans.

It boils down to two basic methods:

1 Take an orphan from an agency, adopt him and raise him as your own.

Many are the older children longing for a home and not chosen because of

their age. (Most people want a baby – with no emotional baggage to deal with.)

Many handicapped children need the loving care of a Christian family. Check with your local social work department about Shared Care. This plan involves your taking a handicapped person for a total of six weeks per year. For this, you are reimbursed several pounds a day for expenses incurred.

If your means allow, consider adopting another child. It will prove an invaluable lesson in sharing for your children as well.

If you cannot take another child permanently, consider taking foster children for weekends and holidays. Your influence might change the course of a life.

2 If adopting another child is beyond your means, then seriously consider adopting a child by mail. All of us can spare ten pounds a month to keep a child from starving.

'Christian Aid', 'Christian Outreach', 'Tear Fund' and others will gladly send you information.

Take it on as a family project to learn about the country where your sponsored child lives. Write him or her letters and send care packages with money your children saved for this purpose.

Teach your children to share and spread God's love at the same time!

Love seeketh not itself to please
Nor for itself hath any care.
But for another gives its ease
And builds a Heaven in Hell's
   despair.

William Blake,
The Clod and the Pebble

Train guide-dogs for the blind

The Guide Dogs for the Blind will pay you to raise a puppy for a year. The dog is then trained as a guide-dog for a blind person.

Perhaps you could take this on as a family project (assuming you have the facilities to keep a dog).

Write to

The Guide Dogs for the Blind Association
Alexandra House
9 Park Street
Windsor Berks SL4 1JR

Service to the helpless

Leona lived alone in a run-down house. She wasn't quite right in her mind. (She fed several mice in her house as pets.) She had been a talented artist but life had dealt her too many blows. Now she couldn't cope.

Her house was in such bad repair that it caused concern among the church people. So a party was organised to fix her porch, her roof and do some painting.

Do you know someone who needs this kind of help? Do you know of a family who could help – yours maybe?

Teach your children love-in-action by helping someone in need of a little time and effort. It may be someone in your church, or someone in your neighbourhood you don't even know. But consider a work project and teach your children the real meaning of love.

You might even want to save coins to fund this project – teaching your children to give unselfishly at the same time.

SOS day

Have you ever heard of a project you wanted to give to financially and wished you had the extra to give? Of course you have.

Well, I'd like to suggest that, as a family, you *earn* the money to give to a worthy cause. How? By a *Sell Our Services* day. How does it work?

1 Announce in your church or neighbourhood that you, as a family, are available for hire for odd jobs. Explain that the money you raise will go to *Oxfam* (or whatever).
2 Choose a day you will give in service. Schedule your jobs with friends.

3 Do some leaf-raking, window washing, garage cleaning or whatever, as a family.
4 Donate the pay to your cause.
5 Praise your children for their sacrificial giving of their time and money. (Then, very quietly, praise yourself.)

Errands for the elderly

Another worthy project that is much needed in most towns is a volunteer errand service to the elderly. Imagine your family typing up notices and delivering them to elderly neighbours or church friends, saying that you will do errands for them *free of charge*. What a great gift to those who cannot do everything for themselves! And what a fantastic way of teaching your children to give of themselves to others!

1 Type up a notice and deliver to those nearby.
2 Clearly list errands within your power to perform: food shopping, mail at post office, picking up prescriptions, etc.
3 Clearly list anything you *cannot* do, so no requests for this service arise.
4 Offer certain hours or days when your services are available – also say when you're *not* available.
5 Explain that no payment will be cepted – that you do this in obedience

61

to Jesus (who exhorted us to care for the widow, the orphan, the poor and the helpless).

6 Include your phone number and any other relevant information.

7 Discuss the project thoroughly in your family and assign various tasks. That way, disputes will be avoided over whose turn it is to . . .

8 Serve joyfully 'as unto the Lord'.

7 The *only* basis for self-worth

'God created me out of pure love . . . From all eternity God thought of me . . . and I had a place in the thought and heart of the eternal God'.

The Spiritual Exercises of St Ignatius of Loyola

THIS is the value God places on each of us and THIS we must teach our children.

St Ignatius goes on to say that no one else can take our place and that we are infinitely valued by God. Doesn't that make you tingle with delight? Don't you want your children to experience this delight too?

We teach our children their value every day. But what kind of value? Little or great?

We teach them they are of little value when we ignore them or their opinions. We teach them they are of no consequence to God when we call them stupid and denigrate their accomplishments. But God would have parents praise their children and delight in their progress.

Maybe the reason we devalue our children is that we aren't too sure of our own worth. Test yourself: When was the last time you felt really good about yourself? Why? When was the last time you felt really lousy about yourself? Why?

If we have grown up feeling we are of little value, we will surely pass that on to our children (and they to theirs).

Drink deeply of these words of St Ignatius. Practise thinking of yourself as very important to God and very loved. Read Psalm 139 and commit these ideas to memory. Then pass this attitude along to your children: that God loves them and accepts them as they are – and that *you do too*!

Then implement some of the ideas in this chapter to cement this knowledge of God's love and acceptance. Set your children free to love and be loved!

Family communication is possible?

'You are so forgetful!' (clumsy, fat, silly, stupid, hopeless, skinny, impolite, sloppy, dull, etc., etc., etc.).

How you speak to your children is either building self-esteem or destroying it.

Many books have been written on this subject, but I cannot emphasise enough how children need to *feel free* to talk with their parents.

Their thoughts are immature, unconventional and usually emotional, rather than logical. But *they are only children*. They need to work out what they think by talking to a caring and patient parent. A few guidelines to aid you in this process:

1 Make yourself available for

communication but don't try to force it. If they know you are available, they'll come to you. (If you are busy when they come to talk, either drop what you are doing or make a definite appointment within the next 24 hours.)
2 Listen, don't talk. They don't want YOUR answers. They'll probably arrive at the same answers eventually, but in their own way and their own time.
3 Don't give advice, unless asked and then not often. Say instead, 'What do you think you should do?' (They usually know, they just have to decide.)
4 Don't make value judgements, like the ones mentioned in the opening lines. You may ONLY say 'I don't like it when you leave a mess', NOT 'You are a messy person'. Confine yourself to 'I feel . . .' and you will be safe. NEVER use 'You are . . .', 'You always . . .', or 'You never . . .'.
5 Be sure your talk and your walk agree. Kids can spot a phoney in a minute. Never profess what you aren't living before your children.
6 Ask questions that require more than a no or yes. Encourage them to think by asking, 'How do you think X will affect Y?'
7 If you think your child is bothered by something and needs to talk, suggest a walk or an outing to provide a relaxed atmosphere for easier communication.

8 If your child divulges some behaviour you don't like, do NOT react. Listen. Know it's a phase. Pray. (If you overreact, you will lose all the rapport you have worked to develop.)

You can build your children's self-esteem just by allowing them to express themselves freely. (Imagine how you would feel if every time you said anything, someone told you it was silly to think that way.) Let them grow and become the unique individuals God created them to be.

Little Jesus, wast Thou shy?
Once and just as small as I?
And what did it feel to be
Out of heaven and just like me?

Frances Thompson,
The Poems of Frances Thompson

An easy supper for a child to prepare

Some busy day or just a day when you have a bored child (of ten or more) on your hands, let that child fix supper for you, for a change.

You not only get a night off, but self-esteem is built by developing skills.

Don't forget to praise him (No matter how it turns out!).

Pitta pizzas

On top of whole pitta bread ovals, spread tomato sauce of purée. On top of that, sprinkle any of the following:

chopped onions	oregano
browned mince	sliced mushrooms
(or sausage or pepperoni)	olives
chopped green peppers	any other favourite
garlic salt	pizza topping

Top with grated cheese and grill or place in the oven for ten minutes, until the cheese melts.

Potato salad

1 Scrub and cut potatoes into chunks without peeling. Boil until tender (about 15 minutes).
2 Hard boil an egg (or two for a large amount).
3 Chop up onions, peppers, celery, pickles and place in a large bowl.
4 When potatoes and egg(s) are done, place in the bowl with chopped veggies.
5 Add 2-3 dessertspoons of mayonnaise and a tablespoon of American-style mustard.
6 Mix and eat hot.

Yoghurt yummy

1 Place enough yoghurt for the whole family in a bowl.
2 If it is shop-bought or already flavoured, you need not add anything to sweeten it. If it isn't, add one tablespoon of your favourite jam.
3 To the sweetened yoghurt, add the following (in whatever amounts you like best): coconut, chopped nuts, half a teacup of porridge oats, chopped fruit (fresh or tinned), raisins, a dessertspoon of wheat germ, a teaspoon of vanilla flavouring, and anything else good you can think of!
4 Mix all together and leave in the fridge to chill until it's time to eat it.

Letters of appreciation

Dear Mom,
Thanks for all you do for me.
Love, Angel

Yesterday, Angela, 12, stayed home from school ill. I was having a particularly busy day trying to write and meeting interruptions at every turn. But I went out to buy yoghurt for her upset tummy. A little while later, Angela came to me with a bracelet she had hidden for me at Christmas and then forgotten, and the above note. Needless to say, it made my morning.

Have you ever received a letter of appreciation from one of your own family? It's truly a special treasure. (I've saved several of these notes from Angela.)

Brighten up an ordinary day for your spouse or child by writing a letter listing five things you appreciate about that person. (I once wrote such a list to my Mom and she was ever so pleased.)

Say those things you find it hard to say without embarrassment or a special occasion to motivate you.

Try to concentrate on characteristics of the person rather than what they do for you: NOT 'I appreciate that you cook well', but 'I appreciate your compassionate nature'.

This is especially good for children who may not know what their best qualities are. (None of us ever hears too much praise anyway.) It builds self-esteem and reinforces good habits already begun.

Don't forget your spouse. He needs praise for being a good father and provider or . . .

Silhouettes

To chart the growth of a child, make silhouettes each year.

It not only produces a picture of them, it says you care – and that says loud and clear 'I am a valuable person'.

To make a silhouette:

1 Tape a large piece of white paper up on a wall.
2 Set your child on a chair square in front of the paper but 3 or 4 feet away from the wall.
3 Shine a bright light from the side – across the child, toward the wall where the paper hangs.
4 The silhouette can then be traced lightly with a pencil on to the paper.
5 Take the paper down and carefully cut around the silhouette.
6 Now cut out a second silhouette of black paper.
7 Mount the black silhouette on a new piece of paper and frame as desired.

Produce a silhouette each year to keep a record of your child's development. (They make great gifts for grandparents too!)

How Mum and Dad married

To increase feelings of belonging and security in your children, choose an appropriate time to tell how you and your spouse met, fell in love and married.

Emphasise how you wanted to have a family – wanted each child – and include as many details of each pregnancy, birth and babyhood as possible.

Your children will love hearing the details. But more than that, it will produce a sense of their own value in them – that they were wanted and loved. Don't be surprised if they ask to hear the story again and again.

(You can even use this opportunity to discuss God's plan for love, marriage and family if time allows. Do make time.)

Another idea is to discuss previous family generations (as accurately as you can). This, too, furthers a sense of belonging and value.

Promise jar

For those times when disappointments come or egos have been damaged by thoughtless remarks, rebuild self-esteem in this way.

Remind your child that you, and God, always think she is special. So keep a 'special moments' jar of Bible promises and peppermints.

Find around the house or at a jumble sale, a large, clear glass jar. Fill this with tiny scrolls of coloured paper on which you have written a Bible promise. Promises should be chosen carefully to offer reassurance of God's love and acceptance of us. Example: 'I will keep you as the apple of mine eye'. (This is not the time for commands to obedience.) Tie scrolls with a colourful bit of embroidery floss or wool.

Throw in among the promise scrolls, peppermints. Then, when the need arises, allow your child to pull out a promise and a peppermint.

Hold your child tightly and read the promise aloud, reminding her that God always keeps His promises. Then give her a peppermint and a hug to smooth over life's bumps.

Take your child to work with you

If you want to make your daughter feel important, as well as better understand you as a parent, take her to your place of work. Show her your work area, job responsibilities and workmates.

Obviously, this may pose difficulties on a normal day, but hopefully you can choose a day off or go after hours, if necessary.

Your daughter will feel ever so grown up, being allowed to experience your adult world for a while. In addition, you're offering an example of your

willingness to be known. Children need to see their parents as people with needs and likes, not just as authority figures. Where else are they to find good adult role models if not in you?

Yearly tape recording

Another memory-maker to turn into a tradition is yearly recordings. What's a yearly recording? Tape an interview with each child on their birthday every year. Ask them what were their favourite happenings in the past year, changes they've made, dreams they cherish for the future. Then save the tapes. They'll remember feeling special

and they'll love hearing them again in ten years!

Blank books

At the beginning of each year (or on every birthday) buy a blank book for children ten and up to record their impressions of life. The year, life, God or you, may all end up in these private chronicles. But in the process, they'll actually be developing themselves by putting their feelings on paper. (It also fosters ability to express yourself.)

As they re-read, what they wrote six months ago will suddenly sound silly or childish. They'll try out various theories of life here, privately, and learn about themselves by having thought it out on paper.

Don't bother to ask about any of this process. It's far too private. Just pray over these blank books and let them grow.

Incentive chart

If teaching a particular child responsibility has proved difficult, try an incentive chart.

For example: Angela's job is to feed the dog, but she forgets and Mum does it to keep the dog from starving.

How to help her remember?

1 Take a large piece of card or sugar paper.
2 Mark it off in squares representing days – no more than two months total. (Children can't handle large blocks of time.)
3 Every seventh day, mark in some small reward (a sweet or 10p). You may draw in a point system as well: each day = x points. But however you choose, arrange for her to work toward small weekly goals and a larger reward (some toy or activity she desires greatly) at the end of the month (or two months).
4 Give her the weekly reward upon remembering seven times and the larger reward at the end of the chart. By the time the end goal is accomplished, the habit should be established, her self-esteem boosted, and the dog thriving.

Do you think your child is a winner?

You can boost your child's self-esteem by encouraging him to enter contests. If you think he is as able an artist as other seven-year-olds, encourage him to enter that drawing contest. He will feel important and capable even if he doesn't win – because YOU thought he could draw well.

Cadbury's sponsors both an art and a poetry contest each spring for children up to the age of 17. While the competition would certainly be stiff, why not encourage your child to enter? The effort of competing will build character and self-esteem no matter who wins.

For further information, write to:

Cadbury's National Exhibition
of Children's Art
Granby School Lane
Dunham Massey
Altrincham
Cheshire
WA14 5SZ

8 Home is where the cook is

'Better a meal of vegetables where there is love, than a fattened calf with hatred.'

Proverbs 15:17, NIV

Kitchens conjure up memories of a warm room, delicious smells and sharing. I spend a lot of time with my family in the kitchen – cooking, eating, washing up, cleaning or just talking. For this reason, I believe the kitchen is the most important room in the home.

If this is so, then capitalise on it by making the kitchen appear sunny and inviting (as well as neat and tidy).

If your kitchen is large enough, add an easy chair, flower arrangements and artwork. Make it aesthetically appealing *and* functional.

If you are not fond of cooking, adding 'eye appeal' to this work area can't hurt. And if you do enjoy hours in the kitchen, you will doubly appreciate the added beauty.

But whether or not you like to cook, your children still need

a place of warmth for sharing
basic lessons in cooking (see below)
a place to experiment and create memories of delicious aromas and closeness with Mum.

So take a close look at your main gathering place, kitchen or wherever else it may be. Has it a comfortable atmosphere? Is it as creative and artistically appealing as you could make it? Does it invite sharing and togetherness? If not, get busy!

I do not mean expensive decor. Rather, plants, children's and other artwork, beauty in any form!

Kitchen inclusions

She watches over the affairs of her household and does not eat the bread of idleness.

Proverbs 31:27. NIV

Some ideas to maximise enjoyment of your time in the kitchen!

1 Place a family noticeboard in the kitchen. Use it to leave love notes, assign jobs, write reminders and include a cartoon or two.
2 Place a helpful verse or two of Scripture on a card above the sink (or wherever you spend the most time) in the kitchen to memorise while you're creating.
3 Use mental time in the kitchen to plan menus ahead (to save time later). Jot down ideas and tack them on your notice board. (I love to cook but I hate to *decide* what to cook. Planning several days (or weeks?) ahead saves the mental energy of deciding each day.)
4 If you have a freezer, organise family cooking sprees. Cook up double or triple portions of soups, casseroles, baked items and freeze them for busy days. Good projects for family cooking

include chili, soups, stews, breads of all kinds, biscuits (especially helpful at Christmas or for parties), fudge, toffees, casseroles and main dishes.

5 Keep an eye on shopping by making a list of staples and ticking items when you need them. Such as

oats	honey
wholemeal flour	syrup or treacle
white flour	powdered milk
brown sugar	potatoes
wheatgerm	dried fruits
oil	raisins or currants
dry beans	spices and herbs
split peas	nuts
shortening	seeds

Buy these items in volume and store – saving initial cost, and time spent in the actual going to the shop and picking them all up several times. (We even go to a separate shop where we get all our staples at one time.)

To help little ones learn to cook

Begin with simple safety lessons:

1 Show a five- or six-year-old (you know your children and can judge when they are mature enough) how to turn on the cooker, and hold her hand near enough the flame or heat to feel the heat but not be burned. Explain how painful a burn is by using sunburn as a comparison.

2 Show him or her how you never leave pot handles turned out toward the front of the cooker.

3 Keep a container of bicarbonate of soda near the cooker and explain that if there ever was a fire, throwing this on the flames would put it out.

4 Next, explain measurement by allowing your son or daughter to play with cups and water in the kitchen sink while you are cooking.

5 Move on to measurement on your scales. It's a great maths lesson at the same time!

6 Give a demonstration of breaking eggs, beating eggs, adding ingredients one at a time, etc.

7 Show how to knead properly. And how to roll dough out – going one direction and then the other with the rolling pin.

8 Show how to line pans with grease or greaseproof paper.

9 Invest in a small kitchen timer and teach them how to set it. Timing properly can be difficult for children who are easily distracted. (They don't need the disappointment of ruined experiments right at the start – and you don't want to waste the ingredients!)

The Good Housekeeping Children's Cook Book is great in that it gives lessons on how to use a knife, how to use the cooker, a dictionary of cooking terms and equivalents.

Gingerbread men

Set oven to gas mark 3, 325°F

1 lb. plain flour	4 oz. margarine or butter
¼ teaspoon salt	8 oz. brown sugar
2 teaspoons bicarbonate of soda	4 tablespoons treacle
	1 egg
1 teaspoon cinnamon	2 teaspoons powdered ginger

Heat, but don't boil, the margarine, brown sugar and treacle. Knead and roll out to approximately ½ cm thickness (more if you want them pudgy). The dough tends to be sticky so roll out on a well-floured board and consider this a lesson in patience. Bake for 20 minutes.

Ice on clothing with icing sugar – coloured of course!

Tip: you can make an icing bag by rolling any piece of paper into a cone and snipping off the end with scissors. Then control icing flow with your finger. (But don't lick your fingers until you're finished.)

Gingerbread men are a must!

Gingerbread men are a great favourite with children – to make and to eat. They also make great gifts. You can dress them up by tying ribbon around their necks and lining gift boxes with coloured foil. The recipe opposite is tried and true. This recipe is particularly good for allowing preschoolers to help. They can do the cutting out once you have the dough in good order.

Tip: The thinner you roll the dough, the crispier they come out. The fatter you make them, the cakier and chewier they become. Take your pick!

When you don't have it – substitute – or make your own!

Many expensive items can be made in larger volume for less money. Such as

Hot Cocoa Mix

2 lb. powdered milk
4 oz. cocoa
12 oz. sugar

Mix ingredients together and keep in an airtight container. Use 1½ tablespoons per cup of milk, or milk and boiling water combined.

Whipped topping

1 well-mashed banana
1 egg white
sugar to taste

Sounds strange, but try it!

Sweetened condensed milk

3 fl. oz. hot water
6 oz. sugar
10 oz. powdered milk

Mix and refrigerate for 24 hours to flavour.

Substitute for an egg

2 tablespoons vinegar
1 tablespoon baking soda

Make your own yoghurt

Use a yoghurt maker or do it yourself, but in either case don't miss out on the health benefits. The commercially sweetened stuff contains too much sugar!

12 oz. powdered milk
3 pints warm water
1 can evaporated milk or
    16 oz. scalded milk
1 carton plain yoghurt
    (with active cultures)

Blend all ingredients together. Heat but do not boil, then cool to approximately 43-49°C. Incubate for several hours by setting in a pan of warm water in a very slow oven.

You can use yoghurt instead of cream, soured cream or buttermilk, or mix it with jam or granola and eat it on its own. (It's great for mild digestive disorders, too.)

Granola (or muesli) – yum!

Set oven to gas mark 4, 350°F

4 oz. vegetable oil
8 oz. margarine
2 tablespoons molasses
1 tablespoon vanilla essence
8 oz. brown sugar
8 oz. honey
½ teaspoon salt

Melt all ingredients in a roasting tin, and stir. When cooled slightly, add

2 lb. rolled oats
4oz. sesame seeds
6 oz. (or more) chopped nuts
8 oz. wheatgerm
8 oz. dessicated coconut
6 oz. sunflower seeds

Stir thoroughly and bake in a roasting tin for 30 minutes, stirring every few minutes.
After granola has cooled, you can add

10 oz. currants or raisins
snippets of dried fruit

Store in an airtight container. It's worlds better than the shop-bought stuff!
Granola can be used in biscuits, as a topping on fruit crumbles or as a topping for cold fruits and ice cream. you need not save it just for breakfast!

Yoghurt ice lollies

Stir together

1 pint plain yoghurt
6 tablespoons (½ small can) frozen orange juice concentrate
1 teaspoon vanilla

Freeze in moulds or small waxed paper cups. Insert sticks into cups when partially frozen.

All the above recipes are easy and fun: children will enjoy helping and eating!

Filling your family or feeding them?

A woman can throw out as much with a spoon as a man can carry in with a shovel.

Old Amish saying

Think about it. Many food items occupy a lot of bulk – until you cook them. Then their size is greatly reduced. So every spoonful of waste is far more than it appears.

Likewise every filling food is not necessarily nutritious. Many menus, planned on busy days, merely fill stomachs, with little nutritional value. We owe it to God and our families to think carefully what we are eating. 'You are what you eat' is not just a funny saying. Our very health depends on a few extra minutes in the kitchen.

Look at the following comparisons and consider buying fewer ready-to-eat items.

Ready to eat (expensive)	Healthier (economical)
sugary cereals	oatmeal, musesli (homemade)
processed meats	
meats	vegetable sandwich
frozen pizza	fillings, cheese, eggs,
bought white	beans, grains
bread and cakes	homemade pizza
ice cream	with wheat crust
bought biscuits	wholewheat or
'heat and serve'	home-made bread
meals	fruit breads
	fruit salads and
	yoghurt
	healthy, homemade
	ones, pasta and
	veggies

Not only are the items in the right-hand column healthier, they are much cheaper! Try it and see. (You'll see fewer trips to the doctor as well.)

Our basic supper menu now consists of:

a hearty vegetable dish (occasionally with a small bit of meat)

fruit/yoghurt   fruity breads

And no one complains about not getting full or lack of meat. (But the transitions must be done gradually. You might begin by cutting out meat two days a week.)

It is very nice to think
The world is full of meat and drink
With little children saying grace
In every Christian kind of place.

Robert Louis Stevenson, 'A Thought'

DID YOU KNOW . . .

that people in Third World countries such as Ethiopia, India and Haiti, spend 70-80 per cent of their income on food, and still go hungry? We are indeed blessed.

Shape your life

Biscuit cutters shouldn't be used only for biscuits, you know. Many things can be cut out just for the fun of it. Such as

scones
leftover bits of pastry
homemade bread dough
(roll thin, cut out and then let rise)
homemade pastas
oatcakes

And why not even cut out pieces of bread to make shaped sandwiches? Animal or star-shaped sandwiches would probably go down faster with slow-pokey 4-year-olds. (Save the crusts for making bread pudding.)

Experiment to see how many foods you can make look like their source.

1 Shape fried eggs into egg shapes. Or cut bread for egg sandwiches into egg shapes.

2 Shape tuna fish sandwiches into fish shapes.
3 Create cow shapes when making beefburgers.
4 When baking bread, all sorts of shapes can be cut from dough before rising.

Healthy snacks

Deciding in which chapter to include this list wasn't easy, since snacks are always in demand on holidays, rainy days and family nights – as well as every other day. But here it is:

apples
bananas
carrot sticks
celery sticks (spread with cheese or peanut butter)
cherry (salad) tomatoes
wheat crackers
biscuits made with whole grains and fruits
dates
dried apples (simply cut and dry in a slow oven)
real fruit juices (frozen into ices)
muesli and muesli biscuits
honey on wheat crackers or bread
nuts
oranges and satsumas
peanuts and peanut butter on whole-meal toast or oatcakes
popcorn
sunflower seeds (available in health food shops)
raisin and nut and seed mixtures
yoghurt

Dress up your salads in style!

To save money on salad dressings, make your own! They are quite simple really. Here are just a few ideas:

Thousand Island

Combine

8 oz. mayonnaise
3 oz. Branston pickle
2 hard-boiled eggs, chopped
2 tablespoons each finely chopped onion and green pepper
1 teaspoon paprika
½ teaspoon salt

Green Goddess

8 oz. mayonnaise
4 fl. oz. yoghurt
2 tablespoons lemon juice
2 tablespoons snipped chives
2 tablespoons snipped parsley
¼ teaspoon salt

Basic vinegar and oil dressing

2 tablespoons vegetable oil	minced onion basil
2 tablespoons vinegar (or lemon juice or combination)	oregano chopped parsley chopped chives
Add to taste:	poppy seeds celery seeds
salt and pepper	
mustard powder	
crushed garlic	

Fresh fruit salad dressing

Beat well 2 eggs. Pour into a saucepan and add 4 oz. sugar, 6 fl. oz. pineapple juice and 2 tablespoons of lemon juice.

Cook over a low heat, stirring constantly until thick. Chill. Yummy!

Gifts from your kitchen

What can you create in the kitchen that would make an acceptable *gift*? Well, I guess it depends on your definition of acceptable, but I enjoy receiving homemade

jams and conserves
dried flowers and pot-pourri sachets
home canned fruits and vegetables
herbed oils and salad dressings
master baking mix (see below)
cheese ball (see below)

pickles and relishes
Breads – plain and fruity ones
lemon butter (see below) or garlic or herbed butter
muesli (see above)
baked goodies of all sorts
dried spices
dried fruits

Lemon butter

4 oz. butter
1 tablespoon grated lemon peel
½ teaspoon basil
1 teaspoon parsley
½ teaspoon chives
½ teaspoon lemon juice

Cream together all ingredients, and pack into small decorative container. Keep refrigerated until needed. Let warm to room temperature for best flavour before using.

Master baking mix

This multi-purpose mix can be made in either 8 lb. or 4 lb. lots. It stores indefinitely so you may as well make lots and give some away to some busy working mum you know.

5 lb. flour (plain or white and wholemeal mixed)
12 tablespoons baking powder
3 tablespoons salt
1 tablespoon cream of tartar
4 oz. sugar
2 lb. vegetable shortening
16 oz. powdered milk

Stir dry ingredients well. Cut shortening into mixture until crumbly and well mixed in. Store in an airtight container.

How to use?

Pancakes

1 egg
8 fl. oz. milk
8 oz. Master Mix

Scones

6 oz. Master Mix
3 fl. oz. milk

Muffins

1 egg
8 fl. oz. milk
2 tablespoons sugar
12 oz. Master Mix

Note: You can also use as crumb topping on fruit crumbles, shepherd's pie, in quiches (no need to make a crust, it forms on its own).

Cheese ball

8 oz. cream cheese
1 lb. sharp cheddar cheese, grated
¼ teaspoon garlic salt
2 tablespoons finely minced onion
½ teaspoon salt
3 oz. chopped nuts

Let cheeses come to room temperature. Combine everything except half the nuts. Form into a ball or log. Sprinkle with your favourite spice and roll in remaining nuts. Chill until ready to serve.

Option: You can add any spice you like to the above mixture to make it curried cheese ball, etc.

For gift giving: wrap in cling film, then in coloured foil and tie at top with ribbon. Or fill a basket with cheese ball, biscuits nuts and fruits for a tasty Christmas present!

Kitchen remedies

It's amazing how we have forgotten all the commonsense (and cheap) remedies to be had right at our fingertips. Here are just a few I've found:

Headache: Two cloves in hot tea. Sip slowly.
Woozy stomach: combine

1 teaspoon bicarbonate of soda
1 squeeze of lemon juice
1 glass water

or try plain yoghurt or fast an entire day (to cleanse the system).

Wart: Spit on the wart and rub with the head of a red-tipped match.

Insect bites: rub with vinegar.

Sunburn: rub with vinegar, or rub with a paste of water and bicarbonate of soda.

Canning and preserving

(For those who grow their own vegetables and love saving money.)

Almost everyone has tried their hand at jam of some scrumptious flavour. But the mere thought of preserving anything else scares off all but the most hearty.

Is it so complicated? Do you need tons of expensive equipment? Not at all. I preserve tomatoes and apples when they are in season and plentiful, with little or no extra equipment.

If you have a freezer, it's easier still. Simply cook tomatoes with nothing added but a little salt until they are mushy. Cool and ladle into plastic bags. Tie up and place in freezer on a tray. (Frozen flat on a tray, they take up less room.)

Apples may be done the same way. Cook with as little or as much sugar as you like and a bit of cinnamon. Cool. Place in bags or old ice cream containers if you have lots of space in the freezer. (We were told of an apple tree on the university campus that no one ever harvested. Now, two years in a row, we've picked up all the apples we could use for free.)

Preserving takes a bit more time, but not much. Follow the same food preparation process. But at the same time, heat jam or mayonnaise jars (or look for 'Kilner' preserving jars at a hardware shop) upside down in a shallow pan of boiling water. (This sterilises them and also heats them enough to keep them from cracking when hot food is poured in.)

When tomatoes are cooked, don't cool. Ladle into hot jars while tomatoes are still boiling hot. (You'll have to hold the jar with a cloth as it will be too hot to touch.)

Wipe off the rim of the jar with a clean cloth. Place lid on and screw on as tightly as possible. Then simply set aside to cool. You're finished! The whole process shouldn't take more than an hour.

Tip: Tomato skins will slide off and not need peeling, if you pile the tomatoes in the sink and pour boiling water over them.

WARNING: YOU CANNOT DO THIS PROCESS ON VEGETABLES WITHOUT ACID – such as carrots or potatoes or peas. For other vegetables (corn, string beans, peas), you must use a pressure cooker and a much more involved process.

Useful books

Learning to cook

Good Housekeeping Children's Cook Book, Ebury Press, London, 1981.
Cooking Is Easy, **Ann Thorpe**, Hamlyn. (For ages ten and upwards; colour pictures.)
Vegetarian Cooking for Children, **Rosamond Richardson**, Piatkus Books, 1986. (Too advanced for children alone. They will need adult help.)
Let's Cook it Together, **Peggy Brusseau**, Thorsons, 1986. (With this book also, children will need help from adults.)
Cooking is Fun, **Ursula Sedgwick**, Hamlyn, 1967. (For 7–12-year-olds, junk food kids' favourites, great visual layouts.)

Other books

Pennsylvania Dutch Cooking, Conestoga Crafts Product, Gettysburg, PA., 1978.
More With Less Cookbook, Lion Publishing, Herts, 1987.
The Busy Mum's Baking Cookbook, **Wendy Craig,** Hamlyn, 1985.
Waste Not, Eat Well, **Maggie Black**, Michael Joseph, 1976.

9 Rainy day possibilities

As I sit to write about rainy days, there's a gale lashing aginst my windows. Yet here am I, cosily tucked away in a Franciscan friary at Almouth, Northumberland, complete with sleeping cat on my feet. The rest of the world hates it, I'm sure, but it's just the sort of day I needed to drink tea and write a rainy chapter. There's nowhere I'd rather be, but it's hardly the same as being at home with an energetic five-year-old trapped indoors by rain.

So what *do* you do with children trapped indoors on rainy days? Basically, you give up accomplishing your 'list' and play with them. Failing that option, you spend half an hour getting them started on a project, and *then* attack your list.

The best strategy is to plan ahead for rainy days. Accumulate rainy day supplies and project ideas. The following pages will outline some ideas. But first, you need equipment. What sort of supplies do I mean? Wonderful things like

empty boxes
ice cream or other plastic containers
glue (or paste for the very young)
shaped macaroni (bought just for artwork)
sugar paper
leftover computer paper
odd wool scraps
paints
crayons and coloured pencils
scraps of cloth
felt-tip markers
wallpaper sample books
old magazines and catalogues
old Christmas cards
children's safety scissors
old socks, for puppets
empty egg cartons
shells and rocks
plastic bottles

Anything and everything can be useful if you let children freely create. They don't think in our conventional patterns. They don't need model kits, just give them odd bits you'd throw out and they spend hours experimenting.

Crafty half-hour fillers

1 watercolour painting
2 bean or shell mosaics
3 potato printing
4 soap carving
5 pressed flower cards
6 baking dough creations (recipe below)
7 junk sculpture (from empty boxes, etc.)
8 string art (wound around nails driven randomly in a wooden board)
9 doll furniture (from matchboxes)
10 doll clothes (glued or sewn)
11 greeting cards

12 collages
13 making up cards for new card games
14 making a doll's house from a shoebox
15 personal posters for bedroom walls
16 jigsaw puzzles (made from pictures they've drawn)
17 snowstorms in glass jars
18 badges and cardboard jewellery
19 shell animals
20 shell-topped boxes
21 pet (decorated) rocks
22 mobiles
23 macaroni jewellery (painted and strung on thread)

Baking dough recipe

Set oven to gas mark 5, 375°F

16 oz. plain flour
 8 oz. salt
 ¾ pint water (more, if necessary)

(Recipe can be halved for one child, as it does not keep well.)

Mix ingredients together. Add a few drops of food colouring if desired, or paint it after baking.

Cut out shapes with biscuit cutters or shape by hand. Be careful to keep shapes flat – rounded shapes do not bake well, cracking or breaking apart. Pierce with a drinking straw to make a hole to hang as ornaments.

Bake for 2 to 3 hours or until dough is hardened. Then paint or decorate as desired.

Note: warn children this dough is not to be eaten.

Play dough

My old standby for rainy days (and not so rainy days) is homemade play dough.

It takes only ten minutes to make and lasts months longer than the bought kind.

8 oz. flour
2 tablespoons powdered alum (available from chemist)
¾ pint water
4 oz. salt
1 tablespoon oil
food colouring as desired

Mix together flour and alum. Heat other ingredients to boiling, then stir liquids into dry ingredients. Knead briefly till smooth. Store in an airtight container.

It's much less sticky, doesn't dry out and lasts twice as long – for a third of the price! Plus you can concoct all the odd colours unavailable in the shops. You can't lose!

Baking creation dough

And if you want to bake your creations to make them last, here's a recipe for baking dough creations.

12 oz. flour
 7 oz. salt
 9 fl. oz. water

Mix together. Knead. Then roll out and cut into shapes. Bake at gas mark 2 (300°F) for about an hour. They can then be painted or varnished to seal them and will last indefinitely.

Children's paste

I even found a recipe for children's paste. So try this out too.

8 oz. sugar   1 tablespoon alum
4 oz. plain flour   oil of cloves
2 pints water

Combine sugar, flour and water in a saucepan over boiling water. Cook until thickened, stirring often. Add the alum and cloves, to preserve it. The paste thickens as it sets. Be sure to keep it tightly sealed to make it last its longest.

Plaster crafts

Last year a friend gave Elizabeth a Peter Rabbit mould and a bag of plaster. She and I had fun making lots of Peter Rabbits from that one bag of plaster. It took only a few spoons of plaster and a bit of water. He dried in two hours. And then Elizabeth could paint him with water colours.

We gave lots of Peter Rabbits to her friends for gifts before that one bag of plaster finally ran out.

Peter Rabbit is only one mould of the many available. Plaster crafts are really easy and inexpensive. Try this easy craft with your children.

1 Little handprints can be made in a paper plate full of plaster and dated – a gift for Gran.
2 Use household objects to pour plaster into if you haven't any moulds.
3 Paper plates full of plaster can have scenes painted on them.

Some of these 'creations' may not look like much to you, but children enjoy the process as much as (or more than) the results. We could take a lesson from them . . .

Soap carving

Bars of ordinary bath soap provide inexpensive entertainment with a little bit of supervision (of knives).

Give each child a new bar of soap and your dullest vegetable knife. Rough shapes should be outlined on the bar initially with the knife tip. Then carve away onto newspaper or right over a table.

Then each child can bathe with his own creative soap shape. Easy shapes include

a ship   a house
a whale   a bottle
a Christmas tree   an egg
a Bible   dice
a cross   dominoes
a coin   a cricket bat
a worm   a train

Note: save leftover shavings and squeeze together into a blob which will still be usable for dirty jobs.

More rainy day ideas for children

For young children (under seven)

1 Punch holes around an old greeting card. Provide a length of wool and a darning needle for young ones to sew in and out of the holes. (You can leave wool in for a gift for Gran or take it out for re-use.)

2 Create a bowling alley of empty bottles and a soft ball. Any hallway will do for the alley.

3 A square of sandpaper and scrap lengths of coloured wool make a 'drawing board' for creating scenes. Wool will adhere to the sandpaper, yet lifts off for the next scene.

4 Pipe cleaners can be folded and shaped into small dolls or animals. They will straighten again after mistakes or for reuse.

5 Stories tape-recorded in advance for days like this come in handy now.

6 Masks and faces can be painted on brown paper bags.

7 Create fruit and vegetable 'people' from apples or potatoes.

8 Let small ones 'work' at the sink, measuring and playing in water with a sponge, colander, eggbeater and various sized cups and spoons.

9 If all else fails, fill the bath and give them lots of empty plastic bottles, spoons, plastic cups and a colander.

10 Give them an old catalogue and suggest they make a picture list for Father Christmas.

For older children

1 Peppermint creams and buck-eyes are easy to make and loved by young cooks (recipes below).

2 Making play money for games can be an activity all in itself. Provide notes for children to copy and let them draw and cut out their own to play shops or to replace money lost from other games.

3 A hobby horse can be constructed from an old broom handle, an old sock or two and some yarn. Older children should be able to handle this one all on their own.

4 Old socks and a bit of yarn, sewn into a face, can make a puppet in a hurry.

5 Comics saved from weeks gone by are soon forgotten and enjoyed again on rainy days. (You can also use them for covering books for school or as gift wrap for children's gifts for parties.)

6 A fishing tackle box filled with paints, scissors, glue, tape and paper would keep any child happy for a good while.

7 Stretch an open-weave dishcloth across an embroidery hoop and let children weave with wool pieces and a darning needle. (Teach them to go one direction and then the other with different coloured threads to create a warp and weft.)

8 Provide each child with a folder to save favourite artwork. A good rainy day task would be collecting it all and arranging it in this folder, with descriptions, dates, etc. (And don't forget to decorate the folder itself.)

9 Give them magnets and let them wander the house learning what is attracted and what is not.

10 Create a hopscotch game or marble ring on the carpet with tape.

11 Suggest relay races that must be crawled instead of run. Or set up various relays, carrying peas with a straw or an orange under the chin.

12 Give them a large cardboard box and let them go. They will think of ten uses for it (fort, car, submarine, house, cave, etc.).

13 Develop a secret code for a friend to decode.

14 Write your own crossword puzzle for Dad or a friend to work out.

Projects that may need Mum's help to get started

1 Create a frieze of a Bible story on a long sheet of paper. Help them divide the paper into different sections for each picture.

2 Suggest that they develop their own cartoon character and draw some cartoons. Provide a special notebook and maybe an idea or two.

3 Create a wall-hanging on hessian cloth with felt. The design should be sketched on paper, cut out of felt and glued on the hessian cloth.

4 Make a diorama in a shoebox. First decide the scene, paint on background

and then scour the house for small objects to act as the furniture or props.
5 Build musical instruments from odds and ends found in the 'junk' drawer.
6 Construct mobiles from a coat-hanger, thread or thin wire and whatever (shells, card, etc.).
7 Design a coat of arms and draw onto heavy card. Paint and display.
8 Create a jigsaw puzzle of some favourite picture by gluing onto card. Let dry and then cut (with Mum's help, with a craft knife).

Peppermint creams

8 oz. icing sugar, an egg white and peppermint essence mixed make a wonderful gooey, pepperminty paste. Roll out ¼ inch thick and cut out in shapes. Leave to dry for 24 hours before eating.

Buck-eyes (Conkers)

Mix together 6 oz. icing sugar, 6 oz. peanut butter and 4 tablespoons margarine, and roll into small balls. Chill for about an hour.

Meanwhile melt a chocolate block. Then dip peanut butter balls into melted chocolate on one side only to resemble buck-eyes.

10 Enlarging your horizons

Can I see another's woe
And not be in sorrow too?
Can I see another's grief
And not seek for kind relief?

William Blake, *Lyrical Poems*

Living on another continent for a while teaches you how little you know, outside your 'own little world' (your own nation). You get a glimpse of this by visiting another country, but *living* in another country teaches you how its people view life.

Most of us spare little time to consider how others think in far away lands. They don't affect our lives so why bother?

I happen to have a keen curiosity about how the rest of the world lives and thinks. There isn't anywhere you could name that I wouldn't like to visit and see what life there is like. Thus, I place high value on world awareness.

However, there's another, greater reason for being aware of the world outside our own sphere. The Bible says we are all brothers and sisters belonging to the same Father. We all are accountable to each other. Thus, it matters how we treat each other on this earth which we share.

William Blake captures this idea in the little poem above. How can we see others in need and not 'seek for kind relief'?

What should we do? How can we seek kind relief? The suggestions in this chapter are only a beginning. Your imagination may take you off into far better realms of 'kind relief'. Ask God to show you how to become more 'world aware' and how you can help your brothers and sisters in need.

Operation World

Operation World is the title of an amazing book which is chock full of information on every country in the world. Prepared for use as a prayer diary, it also makes for interesting reading. (It's published by Marc Europe, and is available from the religious sections of bookstores.)

I used it for some months—fascinated at the knowledge I was gathering about nations I never knew existed. It told me about population, industry, crops, location and climate, as well as about churches there and their specific needs.

I truly enjoyed using it. (I gave mine away and haven't bought another yet.)

Several ways you could use this book in your family:

as a prayer diary
as a family focus for conversation each evening at supper
with slides, for visual impact (see 'tour the world from your own home', below)

as a handy reference when children are preparing projects for school for a family study of the churches of the world.

Increasing neighbourhood awareness

> Live I, live I,
> To my Lord heartily,
> To my Prince faithfully,
> To my neighbour honestly
> Die I, so die I.
> Henry Wadsworth Longfellow,
> *Law of Life*

World awareness begins at home – right in your own neighbourhood.

Do you have neighbours you've never met? Or barely remember their names? Have you ever thought of getting together, but didn't know what excuse you could use? Try a neighbourhood party!

1 Winter – an outing such as ice-skating and refreshments at your house.
2 Christmas – a biscuit exchange (where everyone brings two dozen biscuits, eats a few and takes a half-dozen variety pack home).
3 Summer – jumble swap or jumble sale and picnic supper some Saturday.
4 Any time – dinner and Bible study for couples, or
5 Ladies' Bible study and brunch in the morning.

6 Block party – with games, booths, bonfire and sausage roast. (Organise the kids to put on a talent show or circus.)

Don't expect everyone to join in, but any friends you can make are welcome in your life, aren't they?

Adopt a missionary

You can increase your awareness of a single country by establishing a friendship with a missionary.

1 Choose a country you are particularly curious about, or choose a missionary you know and study her country. (If you don't know how to find a missionary to adopt, check with your minister or your denominational headquarters. Or consult the *UK Christian Handbook* (Marc Europe, 1987-8) for mission board headquarters, who will be glad to help you.)
2 Begin by writing to the missionary and informing her of your interest and asking her to answer specific questions your children have about her country. (Be sure to ask if she has children. If so, your children could correspond directly with them. If not, there are probably children nearby she could arrange as pen pals.)
3 Ask her for prayer requests that you, as a family, could remember.
4 Ask her what practical items you could send her or her children / pen pals. Then post a box of inexpensive

items. The money could be raised by a project or saved by the family.

5 Start a missions piggybank for this project or others. Teaching children to save *to give to others* is an excellent lesson in selflessness.

6 Send a magazine subscription or some Christian publication the missionary might enjoy receiving.

7 Ask her to send you any pictorial information on her country that is available. (Be sure to send money to cover the postage costs.)

8 Find books and information at the library on this country, written at your child's level. Then look at the books together.

9 Ask her to send you a picture of her to pin up in some prominent place (on the fridge?) to remind you all to pray for her.

Tour the world from your own home

Check your local library to see what slides of other countries they lend. Children remember what they see and will love seeing slides from other countries.

If you're interested in biblical history and scenery, write to

> Bible Scene Slide Tours
> 26 Home Close
> Sharnbrook
> Bedford
> MK44 1PQ

for slide programmes on the Holy Land.

This organisation specialises in programmes illustrating Biblical history for church and home.

Bible slides woulld make a great family night programme!

Door of Hope

Another family project to foster missions interest in your children is the Door of Hope organisation.

Door of Hope sends Bibles to Iron Curtain countries *with our help*. How can you help?

They operate by sending you portions of Scripture. You mail them to people whose names and addresses they supply. Mine were portions of Luke in Czech which I sent to individuals in Prague. You address the envelopes and pay the postage. This way, Communist authorities can't spot mass mailings, and the people get the Bible one portion at a time.

To include your children, they could earn and/or save pennies for postage stamps.

You could also research one particular Iron Curtain country and educate your children about the freedom we enjoy.

You can contact the Door of Hope at

Box 430	or	Box 303
Windsor		Glendale
Berkshire		California 90323
S14 3TB		USA

The Bible Society reading programme

The Bible Society has developed portions of Scripture in simple language that are used to teach Africans in Chad to read. Many children (and adults) are learning to read by reading the Bible and coming to faith in God at the same time.

You can help by sending money to

> The Bible Society
> Stonehill Green
> Westlea
> Swindon
> SN5 7DG.

A family missions holiday project

Phil's sister and brother-in-law are a nurse and surgeon team. They are also committed Christians, and have three teenagers.

Every spring they fly to Haiti, where they perform needed surgery for nationals. They receive no money for this week (or two weeks). Instead they pay their own expenses.

Why, you ask, would anyone choose to fund a working holiday? Because they want to share the love of Christ by giving their time and expertise to these people who have not the benefits of ample medical care.

Bob and Alice often take along their three teenagers, who roll bandages, stock supplies or do anything else to help. And do the kids enjoy these trips? Yes, they keep going back – despite missing school and not getting the advantages of a 'proper' holiday.

Many Christian families choose to spend their money and holiday time using their skills, giving freely to those who have not.

Some perform surgery. Others build schools, teach English or type for two weeks.

I'd like to suggest that your family consider giving of yourselves to a short-term missions project. Obviously, your children may not be the right ages for such a venture. But you could leave them with Gran.

For more information, contact your denomination's missions department or consult the UK Christian Handbook for other mission boards who will welcome your willingness to build the Kingdom of God.

What an education for your children! What an example of unselfishness! Some blessings are too unusual to miss!

Papua New Guinea experiment!

To increase Third World awareness, find an illustrated book on life in Papua New Guinea. Do a bit of reading and discuss the following experiment with your children. They'll go for it, I'm sure.

1 Plan a summer evening to camp out. Use a tent, if you can get one, or sleep under the stars without a tent (if your area is safe enough).
2 Discuss ahead of time how the people of New Guinea live, and announce plans to spend an evening as they would live.
3 Choose carefully what you can cook over a fire. (No barbecue grills or liquid lighter). Choose foods they would eat if possible – chunks of meat, corn on the cob, raw vegetables, fruit for 'sweets'.
4 Sleep rolled in blankets – no cheating with sleeping bags.
5 Allow no electricity. Use candles or just your firelight. (If you plan the right time of the month, you could have the aid of moonlight.)
6 Discuss the climate, animal life and family life in New Guinea, around your campfire.
7 Go to bed at dark and get up early to correspond with their schedule.

Adopt a foreign student

Among our friends, we are fortunate to know university students from Malawi, Ireland, America, Canada, Cyprus, India and Malaysia. What fun it is to get to know them, their customs and, indirectly, their countries.

Adopt a foreign student from a nearby university (or perhaps a foreign family living here) into your circle of friends. The experience will benefit your entire family. And your friendship could make a major difference to their enjoyment of their stay here.

1 Invite foreign visitors to your church and your home.
2 Invite them to come to your house to cook a meal from their homeland.
3 Share holidays with them and learn of their customs.
4 Visit their homeland, if possible, and learn first hand!

There's so much world to be explored. Make it a family project to investigate as much of it as you can!

Third World meals

Increase your awareness of food in different areas of the world – or of the lack of it.

1 Hold foreign cuisine nights just for the family. Choose Friday as 'foreign food night'. Allow children to take turns choosing a country. Then plan a menu representative of that country. While eating, you can discuss what grows in that climate and what they would *not* have to eat there.
2 I once stayed in a Franciscan friary. I happened to be there on a Friday, to find that lunch was soup – only. (Lunch happened to be the main meal of the day.) Friday's soup luncheon was their way of remembering to pray about world hunger. They not only talked about this need: they went without food to save some of the world's resources. Try this in your family.

3 To make an even stronger impression on your children, serve only rice and water at some meal. When they ask 'Where is the rest of the meal?' you can explain that this is all most of the Third World ever has to eat. Then pray together for these people with so little.

I once entertained a ladies' church group, dedicated to missions. For refreshments, I served only Jacobs' crackers and water. Needless to say, they were not pleased with me. They missed the whole point. I had done it to save money for missions and remind them that we all eat more than we actually need.

So when you try these means of sacrifice, remember this: what we don't eat may leave more for the hungry. It is not our right to overeat, just because we can afford it.

Foreign craft items

For a family night activity, research and make some craft item from a foreign country.

Ideas:

basket weaving – Latin America
weaving or sewing wall
 hangings – Africa
origami – Japan
macramé – South America
pottery – Mexico
painting eggs – Romania
wood carving – Germany
painting on wood – Europe
shell sculpture – Caribbean
tie-dying (fabric) – Africa
batik (dying fabric and using wax)
 – Africa

You might want to study the country and discuss it while completing the project.

Useful books

The *Let's Go to. . .* series published by Franklin Watts. Includes volumes on India, Indonesia, Malaysia, Ethiopia, Saudi Arabia, Japan, England, China, Greece, Sweden, Portugal and more.
Rich Christians in an Age of Hunger, **Ron Sider**, Hodder and Stoughton, 1978.

11 The joys of nature

Dear God,

If you made the sun, the moon and the
stars, you must have had lots of equipment.

Paul

Children's Letters to God,
ed. Eric Marshall
and Stuart Hample, Collins, 1977.

I took a walk along the Lade Braes this morning. The sky was tinted pale blue and the sun was peeking over the ridge dappling the path through the bare trees. A gorgeous January day.

I wished for Elizabeth when I saw a grey heron meditating in the stream. (She was the first to spot him in that same stream a month ago, saying quietly, 'Mummy, there's one of those birds with the long beaks'.)

I couldn't help wondering if his feet didn't ever get cold, standing so still in that icy water. Yet he stood tall and proud and inspired me with his serenity.

Looking behind me, I saw that the 'snowdrop bank' was indeed turning white. The aconites had already made their debut as well, and my heart soared with the joy of spring and of my God.

The words running through my mind came from the Song of Solomon:

See the winter is past;
the rains are over and gone.
flowers appear on the earth;
the season of singing has come,
the cooing of doves
is heard in our land.

2:11-12

As I reluctantly sauntered home, I meditated on God's beautiful creation and its diversity. Again I wished for Elizabeth, who loves nature as much as I. She would have appreciated this perfect morning. I was tempted to go and get her out of school. Surely this was more valuable . . .

I think it is fair to say that I have inspired this reverence for nature in Elizabeth. And I can honestly say I tried to do just that. For it is in these settings that children (and I, His child) meet God.

Do all within your power to offer your children this knowledge of God which He has built into His creation. *Nothing* can replace these experiences.

My very own garden

Even children who don't like vegetables will take an interest in growing their very own.

Try offering your son (or daughter) a garden patch all his own–even if it means digging up some of the grass. Depending on his age:

1 Let him choose anything he wants to grow.
2 Take him to purchase the seeds.
3 Obtain a book from the library and leave it up to him to find out how to cultivate vegetables.
4 Provide the money for seeds and fertiliser.
5 Supervise as little as possible.

It's a great lesson in patience, as well as enjoyment of independence. It also provides opportunity to discuss the miracle of growth, which God included in creation.

Who knows? He might even decide to eat the brussel sprouts he grew!

Family camping basics

God made the country and man made the town.

William Cowper, *The Task*

Roughing it may not be your idea of a relaxing holiday. But your children may never experience the beauty of sleeping under the stars or the feelings of family togetherness in quite the same way.

A weekend camping trip now and then provides the close-up exposure to nature we all need to remind us of God's creativeness. And camping really isn't so complicated. You can get by with the basics and a bit of organisation.

Here's what you need to start:

1 a tent
2 a camp stove or barbecue grill (wood fires are great if you live in a dry enough climate)
3 plastic cups/dishes
4 *simple* menus and food supplies (see below for ideas)
5 drinking water in large jugs
6 a dry change of clothing
7 a washing-up bowl
8 a torch
9 sleeping bags
10 rain gear

11 a camera (for memories)
12 a family game or two
13 a bird and/or wildflower book
14 binoculars

Don't take a radio, a suitcase full of clothes and the kitchen sink. Simplify.

Supper bundles

Place a beefburger in a large piece of aluminium foil. Slice potatoes, carrots, onions on top. Sprinkle with Worcester sauce and wrap up tightly. Make one bundle for each person and place over grill or wood fire for half- to three-quarters of an hour (depending on the fire).

S'mores

Toast a marshmallow and place it and a piece of plain chocolate between two digestives and heat over the fire until chocolate is melted. (Called S'mores because the kids will ask for s'(ome) more.)

Nature theme walks

Camping is the ideal time to take theme walks. Set off in search of butterflies, or birds or wildflowers. Be sure to take along the appropriate bird or flower guide to learn the names of each new variety.

Or centre your entire holiday around walking. Phil and I are just back from a walking trip in North Wales. Walking along a backroad from Conwy to Betws-y-Coed will remain one of the highlights of my life.

We had lovely weather for February (cold but clear) and a view that will forever be etched in my mind's eye. The road ran along a plateau which sloped down into a valley on either side, with mountain peaks on the far side of each valley. A river ran to our left and you could see for miles! Never have I known such peace or such oneness with all God's creation.

And the feeling of freedom was overwhelming as well. Walking involves no schedules, no rush and you can literally take time to enjoy the scenery to the fullest. I'm hooked now. I'll definitely need more.

Many such walks are to be enjoyed – free for the taking. Below I've listed a few books to get you started.

Walking in England, **Roger Redfern**, Robert Hale and Co., 1976.
Walking through the Lake District, **Michael Dunn**, David and Charles, 1987.
Along the Pennine Way, **J.H.B. Peel**, David and Charles, 1979.
Walking through Wales, **David and Kathleen MacInnes**, David and Charles, 1984.
Red Guide books by Ward Lock Ltd.

Star gazing

Camping (or any night) also provides opportunity to star gaze. Again, take along a guide of some sort and read

Psalm 8 to the children as well – to remind them who made the stars.

Beach frolics

You look forward to your holiday at the beach for months. Then *why*, when you get there, is it not all you'd hoped? Why can't the children entertain themselves with all that sand and sea? If 'What can we do now?' is a frequent refrain, suggest

1 your children join with other children on the beach for team competitions in sand castle building
2 team competition treasure hunts (treasure buried in the sand, of course)
3 tennis on hard-packed sand
4 collecting certain types of shells for making jewellery and mosaics at home later
5 digging a pit for a clam bake (you'll have to get some clams first, of course).
6 gathering driftwood for a sausage roast at tea time
7 team volleyball or relay races
8 hopscotch squares drawn in sand
9 binoculars and a bird book to spot new shore birds

Note: Be sure to take along plenty of plastic toys as well as bowls, buckets, spoons and plastic bags for sand play and gathering shells and treasures.

Soil testing

From your local garden centre, obtain some litmus paper to test the acidity of your garden soil. Older children will enjoy testing soil all around your garden – and neighbours' as well.

Consider planting a hydrangea bush, whose lovely blossoms vary from pale pink or pale blue to bright pink, blue or even purple, depending on the acidity of the soil.

Indoor gardens

Even in winter you can enjoy green and blooming things inside. Children love to watch the growth process. Use anything handy to grow indoor plants:

1 Sprinkle cress seeds onto a wetted sponge.
2 Sprout beans or seeds for salads in a clean glass jar, covered with a cloth to let them breathe. Simply soak overnight and then place in the jar. Leave in the dark for 3-4 days or until sprouts are about 1½ inches long. Rinse with warm water once a day. (Alfalfa seeds and mung beans sprout well.)
3 Save the top of a pineapple. Soak in a shallow dish of water for two days. Then plant in potting soil. It gives a lovely tropical look to a room.
4 Carrot tops can be turned into houseplants in the same way.
5 Save tomato, pumpkin or any fruit seeds for children to experiment with sprouting.

6 Make a terrarium (bottled plant garden) out of odds and ends around the house. Find the largest glass jar you own or can find from a friend (to hold at least 5 litres). Layer with several inches of potting soil. Then make a trip to the woods and bring tiny ferns and plants of your choosing to plant in the bottle or jar. You can include small interesting pieces of wood or stones to create atmosphere. Or small animal figurines to delight children. Water well and cover with lid. It shouldn't need watering for months if you don't open it. But you can watch the woods expanding and changing. If any plants don't adapt well, replace with fresh ones.
7 A cactus garden could be created the same way, with sand and little or no water.

Sand candles

Lovely, unusual candles can be made by pouring wax into a well in sand. Here's how:

1 Choose some unusually shaped dish or container and fill half to two-thirds full of clean sand.
2 Melt wax over hot water to liquid state. Colour with broken crayon bits.
3 Dip a length of string into the wax. Remove and let it harden for your wick.
4 With your hands, fashion a well in the centre of the sand – according to the shape of the container, or any way you like. Dampen the sand with water to retain the shape of the well.

5 Slowly and carefully pour wax into the sand well and insert the wick in the centre (or several wicks if you desire).
6 Let wax harden undisturbed.
7 Remove candle carefully from sand and lightly dust off non-clinging bits.
8 Light and enjoy.

U-Pick veggies and fruits

Nature is but a name for an effect, Whose cause is God.

William Cowper,
The Winter Walk at Noon

I recall a hot August day climbing up the trees and dropping warm peaches down to Daddy below me. I was so thrilled that this year he had let me do the tree climbing.

Hot work though it was, I was in my glory with the heady smell of peaches and the fun of this excursion with Daddy. And the delicious adventure of sneaking one now and then . . .

And I remember many such trips to pick strawberries and sneaking *a lot* of those luscious bites.

The combination of the wonderful fruits of God's creation and the closeness of a parent lingers with me years later.

Your children will enjoy going to a 'U-Pick' farm as much as I did.

This summer, find a fruit or vegetable patch nearby and take them along to create this warm and wonderful memory. These farms are more reasonable than fruit and vegetable shops and loads more fun.

Painting mushrooms?

My friend, Bonnie, is a painter. So she used to drag me out to the woods to paint. I say 'drag' because I am *not* an artist and the thought of me going out to paint was a laugh.

However, I found it doesn't take much talent to paint with watercolours. And the time we spent, silent in the woods, was thoroughly refreshing.

Take your children out in the woods – just to *be there*. Take watercolours and let them paint whatever takes their fancy.

Take along a sandwich so you needn't hurry home.

Teach them just to 'be'. Teach them the joy of silence – and they'll learn to commune with God.

Looking back on those expeditions in the woods to paint mushrooms, I long to return. That was a lifetime ago and now too far away but, oh! the pleasure of those memories!

Pony-trekking in the woods

There we were, riding horses through the lovely, wintry woods. What a pleasant memory to cherish! Angela and I will never forget that ride through the woods in the Pocono Mountains of Pennsylvania.

Combine two great joys in life by taking your children pony-trekking in some woody setting. All children love horses and what's not to love about a forest? Check around to see if there's a riding stable near you or a National Park which offers guided pony-trekking.

Farm life

The newborn lamb snuggled up under my chin. Angela held another and Elizabeth ran excitedly back and forth between us, begging to hold both.

A church friend manages a university farm and had taken us for a visit in very early spring. Baby lambs snuggling, piglets squealing, calves nursing and Shetland ponies to ride – a child's heaven!

Check to see if there's a university farm nearby or just a friendly farmer who will allow you to visit occasionally so your children can enjoy a taste of farm life.

Or better yet, plan a farm holiday some summer and live there a few days!

Nature craft classes

Do you know a lot about butterflies or mushrooms or seashells? Could you teach a nature craft class? Then consider offering it to the children in your neighbourhood.

If you regularly take your children on nature walks, bird watching or hunting rare wildflowers, then, with a bit of co-operation, you could teach a children's class.

1 Choose your area of expertise.
2 Announce it to neighbourhood (or church) mothers to see who's interested.
3 Consider a place, cost involved and transportation. Ask the other mothers to help provide whatever you need.
4 Plan the class for a set number of sessions.
,5 Suggest to other mothers that they teach some nature craft of their choosing.

It's a great way to become better acquainted with your neighbours and educate the children as well!

Start a nursery

For plants – not toddlers!
If you love gardening and regularly start your own bedding plants from seed, then why not expand into a business? You could choose to sell them to augment family income or give the profits to charity.

You might just want the joy of giving them away to fill in the church landscaping, to friends and relatives. It really doesn't require much money or time. And your children will love watching the growth process.

1 Ask friends to save flower seeds for you the autumn before you intend to start.
2 Keep the seeds dry and identified in labelled envelopes.
3 About March, plant seeds in yoghurt pots or some other inexpensive container.

4 Keep them warm and well-watered. Allow children to help in every way possible, teaching them the process as you go.
5 Separate the plants when they begin to bear leaves. Keep them grouped so as not to lose identification.
6 Harden off by setting plants outside a few hours at a time, to start with.
7 Plant outside in beds if you have room enough.
8 When ready to sell, simply dig up and wrap in old newspapers.
9 Earmark the money for a specific charity or project to gain maximum satisfaction.
10 Give some to the children to grow as their very own, as a reward for their hard work.

Volunteer landscaping

Do your church grounds need a bit of shaping up? A few weeds pulled or flowers planted does wonders for the appearance of a church.

Why not volunteer your family to landscape around the church? You needn't be professionals to plant flowers or compose a rock garden in a bare corner.

1 Speak to the minister. He'll probably be thrilled!
2 Take a walk around to survey the current condition.
3 Formulate a plan on paper (just to teach your children methodical work habits) and sketch out what will grow where.

4 Buy or borrow appropriate tools.
5 Be sure to take the children with you when you go to buy bedding plants or flower seeds. Include them in every phase of the project.
6 Choose a date and make a day of it – picnic lunch and all – until the job is completed.

I would rather be a 'landscaper' in the house of the Lord . . .

We are God's winter helpers

Winter is hard on birds. Everyone knows that, except children. As a part of teaching children consideration for others, try making birdfood.

Gather:

suet or	a coconut half or
peanut butter	mesh fruit bag
seeds	as a container
nuts	string.

Mould a blob of suet around the middle of a length of string. (Use suet or peanut butter as the glue to hold it all together.) Then roll in bird seed and nuts. (Wet your hands to aid handling without losing half the suet on your hands. Not even children will want to lick suet and birdseed off their fingers!)

Hang the birdfood ball near a window, so children can watch the birds at close range. Keep a bird book nearby to help identify 'strangers'.

Alternatives:

1 Fill a mesh fruit bag with peanuts and hang.
2 Attach peanuts (in shell) to a length of twine by sewing them into a long string with needle and strong thread.
3 Pop popcorn, then string it with a needle onto sturdy thread and hang lengths in nearby trees.

Books to use in nature education

All About the Yorkshire Terrier, **Mona Huxham**, Pelham Books (plus 26 other titles in the 'All About' series).
A Tour of British Bird Reserves, **Valerie Russell**, Crowood Press, 1986.
My Wilderness in Bloom, **Phil Drabble**, Michael Joseph, 1986.
Observer's Guide to Sea Fish, Frederick Warne, 1972 (and many other titles in the Observer's series).
The Fox Terrier, Popular Dog Press, 1965 (and 15 other titles).
Nature series by MacDonald Publishers, London, on Weather; Oceans; Rivers and Lakes.
The Animal Book of Records, **Talus Taylor and Annette Tison**, MacDonald, 1984 (Guinness Book of Records style).
The Hamlyn Guide to the Countryside of Britain and Northern Europe, **ed. Pat Morris**, Hamlyn, 1982 (Fauna and flora, well illustrated).
The Hamlyn Guide to Birds of Britain and Europe, **Bertel Bruun**, Hamlyn, 1970.

12 What is nurture?

Dear God,

We got a lot of religion in our house, so don't worry about us.

Teddy

Children's Letters to God

Cute, huh? But I wonder what Teddy meant by religion . . . did he mean they went to church once in a while? Or that Christ truly lived and ruled in that home?

As parents, our job is far greater than a mere exhortation to 'religion'. I hope to teach my children to *worship* God.

I read a definition of worship that stopped me in my tracks. It was written by Dr William Temple and inspires me each time I read it again. (It's quoted in *Heralds of God* by James Stewart, published by Hodder and Stoughton – I couldn't find the original reference.) The numbering is mine.

To worship is

1 To quicken the conscience by the holiness of God.
2 To feed the mind with the truth of God.
3 To purge the imagination by the beauty of God.
4 To open the heart to the love of God.
5 To devote the will to the purpose of God.

Is this not a worthy goal for parents? Let's look at these five goals individually.

1 To quicken the conscience by the holiness of God. The equivalent parental goal here is discipline. Children must learn somewhere in life that, loving as God is, His holiness will not tolerate sin. So, we teach our children right from wrong and thereby develop a conscience in them. When they are older, they will gain insight into the holiness of God and want to be like Him. Then they won't need a conscience. For now, we must be their consciences for them.

2 To feed the mind with the truth of God. This at first glance appears easier than number 1. However, taking them to church is not sufficient to develop children's knowledge of the truth in the Word of God.

We must also teach them to love truth at home – which means we must set crystal clear examples of honesty before them in our daily actions. No little white lies (there never was such a thing, anyway). No hypocrisy, no laxity in our own search for the truth of who God is. No, it's not so easy, but a worthy goal.

3 To purge the imagination by the beauty of God. I have mentioned

elsewhere my love of beauty and my theory of its influence on my children. Again, I say use every opportunity to impress on your children that ALL beauty originates in God. Everything else in this world is only a shadow, a poor attempt at copying God's infinite imagination. Fill their minds with beauty in every form and they will be simultaneoulsy learning of God.

4 To open the heart to the love of God. There is only one way I know of to do this and that is to love your children *unconditionally* (the way God loves us). You can't spoil children with love, only by lack of discipline.

Think about it. Do you, as an adult, ever feel you get *enough* love? Neither do your children. Build their self-images and their view of God by (1) accepting them for who they are; (2) not trying to change them; (3) praising them; and (4) forgiving 70 x 7 times. People who never know earthly love seldom ever find God's love a reality.

5 To devote the will to the purpose of God. It seems to me that if we, as parents, succeeded with the first four elements in this definition, then the fifth would take care of itself.

For to know God is to love Him. To know His love is to want to devote your will, indeed, your whole being, to His purposes.

Sounds like a tall order? Over-whelmingly so, but don't forget

1 God is there to direct you, and
2 He loves your children even more than you do.
3 You live these principles out day by day over a long time.
4 You will fail, but God is able to redeem our failures and bring good anyway.

Resolve to put these principles into your family life – to nurture your children's minds, self-esteem and view of God.

This chapter contains more seed-ideas for nurture, from which you can pick and choose.

Bedtime stories

Hush, my dear, lie still and slumber,
Holy angels guard thy bed.
Heavenly blessings without number
Gently falling on thy head.

Isaac Watts, *Cradle Hymn*

We give our children a great gift when we send them off to sleep with feelings of security and being loved.

Going to bed should be a pleasure and a time with Mummy and/or Daddy. But how to create this aura of closeness?

Obviously a lot depends on each child, but those reluctant to go to bed are usually craving more time with parents – more reassurances that they are loved.

A few suggestions:

1 Plan bedtime to suit your child, not your evening. Some children require more sleep than others. But if your child seems to be fighting going to bed, consider whether you are putting her to bed earlier than necessary, just to obtain a peaceful evening. If this is the case, she feels cheated of time and affection and gets even with you by fighting – thus spoiling the peace you sought.

2 Regulate your child's body functions by putting her to bed at the same time every night, if possible. She will begin to feel ready for bed at this time.

3 Establish and keep a bedtime routine to add feelings of security. Always reading a story and saying prayers will give your child a feeling of order and completion to the day. Then she knows it is time to sleep because all has been done as usual.

4 Choose a book with a bedtime story for each day of the year if you like. Better yet, send her off to sleep with some thought of God by using a daily devotional such as the 'Simon and Sarah' series by Scripture Union. Or read a Bible story *from a Bible story book* written especially for your child's age.

5 Teach your child the Lord's Prayer as soon as possible. (Children's memories are remarkable!) Teach her also 'Now I lay me down to sleep' and let her pray

in this bedtime routine (teaching her to talk to God for herself even as young as two or three).

6 For a child who is fearful, remind her that you will be nearby all night; but even more importantly, tell her that God watches over us all, since He never needs to sleep.

7 Reassure her of your love with hugs and kisses before leaving the room.

This whole process takes only about ten minutes and can save the child, and you, from hours of crying and fighting going to bed.

For children who still resist, get into bed with them and read stories or allow them to look at books for a few minutes before turning out the light.

Then don't respond to continuous calls for water or whatever else they dream up to get you to come back. Tell them lovingly but firmly that you will be nearby but you will not keep coming back.

You might want to recite either the opening poem or the one below, just before leaving the room

> There's a friend for little children
> Above the bright blue sky.
> A friend who never changes
> Whose love will never die.
>
> Albert Midlane,
> *Good News for Little Ones*

Special events

Whenever your child takes some step forward in spiritual matters, give her some special remembrance of the occasion. This is the time to praise, to congratulate, to motivate her on in this direction.

1 Give her a Bible or some other helpful Christian book.

2 Take her photograph and give it to her framed and dated – as a remembrance of joining the church, for instance.

3 Give each of your children some special remembrance to keep as they make spiritual strides. Ideas for remembrances: fresh flowers which can then be pressed; a rock or shell of particular beauty; a cross on a chain; or even a ring (the circular shape of which symbolises eternity).

Not only will you make a memory, but the psychological affirmation will motivate them further into spiritual realms.

> God be in my head, and in my
>   understanding,
> God be in mine eyes, and in my
>   looking;
> God be in my mouth, and in my
>   speaking;
> God be in my heart, and in my
>   thinking,
> God be at my end, and in my
>   departing.
>
> From a Book of Hours (1514)

103

Bible memorisation techniques

Crazy images

Bible memorisation need not be drudgery. Try spelling out a verse in pictures. Choose your verse and then find sound-alikes

Example:

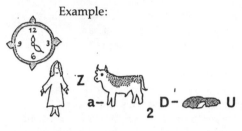

Our God is   able   to de-liver   you

Scripture songs

Set longer Scripture passages to any tune and learn them in five minutes.

Or choose one of the many Scripture song records and learn the songs on the record by singing along: first with a Bible, and then from memory!

Home church service

On the odd Sunday when you are snowed in or some of the children ill, why not have your own church service at home?

1 Let everyone stay home together.
2 Ask each child to choose a song to sing.

3 Tell favourite Bible stories or
4 Ask Dad or Mum to retell a story and apply it to your lives (i.e. a story of illness/healing if there is a sick child, or a story of deliverance if you are snowed in). Be sure to ask discussion questions.
5 Learn a new verse together (see Bible verse memorisation techniques, above).
6 For small children, ask them to draw the story to help fix it in their minds.
7 Close with prayer together (related to the story discussed).
8 Make pancakes or some brunchy menu and share together with hugs.

Seven whole days, not one in seven
I will praise thee;
In my heart, though not in heaven,
I can raise thee.

George Herbert (1593-1632)

Visit other churches

Recently, Angela asked me what it was like to attend a Catholic mass. Instead of trying to describe it, I took her to mass the next Sunday. It didn't happen to appeal to her, but visiting a Catholic church aided her understanding of what the 'church universal' means.

You do your children an injustice if you never take them to visit churches of other faiths.

1 Take them to visit churches of faiths

as opposite from yours as possible – Jewish or pentecostal.

2 Read up on Islam or Buddhism in order to be able to answer their questions.

3 Suggest family studies on a country where the majority of the people belong to a very different faith, such as India and Hinduism.

Educate your children in the 'bigness' of God and the many people who view him differently, and thus, worship Him differently. Then they can better appreciate God and their own church.

Entertaining children in church

Our church in St Andrews sees a lot of tourists in the summer, and I remember one family in particular from last year.

They had four of the most well-behaved children I have ever seen in church. They sat, looking straight at the minister (as if they were truly listening). They had no toys, no snacks to keep them quiet and neither parent had to tell any of them to be still or quiet, for the entire service. I was awed.

Here I sat behind them with a squirmy four-year-old, who may have been quiet, but was certainly not still, and we had a pewful of her favourite books with us.

I couldn't help but wonder what these parents had done with these children, ranged from about ten down to three years of age, to get them to sit so well in church. (Do they threaten to beat them black and blue? I wondered.)

Many may disagree with my methods, but I want my girls' earliest memories of church to be pleasant ones. Now since I didn't get to ask those parents their secret, I must still rely on my own means of making these early church memories pleasant.

My girls were in church both services every Sunday from about two weeks of age. I didn't want to miss church for several years until they could behave, so I had to teach them (early) about God's house.

So I held them as babies and missed about half of the service's content. But I still liked to think that my babies were absorbing the atmosphere of worship.

As each grew older and squirmier, I took small (quiet) toys or books.

After they got beyond the choking stage, I took raisins to feed them when they got restless.

As the pastor's wife, my children were favourites in the church, and often someone else would volunteer to have one sit with them. The change always resulted in better behaviour.

When they got to three or four, I let them choose which (quiet) toys they wanted to take to church.

I never did a lot of talking about 'this being God's house, so you have to be quiet'. I don't like the implication that God must always be placated by proper behaviour. But I did tell them that church was a special place and that to be polite, we must be quiet so everyone could hear.

Elizabeth, five, is usually the only child under 15 at our evening service of 250 people. (The other mothers stay home since there is no crèche.) She goes armed with books and often 'favours' someone different with her presence, sitting quietly looking at books. Or she sits snuggled up to me, enjoying my closeness as I caress her face and hair.

I wouldn't miss these moments for anything. And I believe these times serve to foster her love of church and, ultimately, of God.

I can remember sitting in church at about four. Someday, as she sits in church with her child, so will she.

Prayer partners in your family

Family unity is cemented rapidly by linking up family members for prayer.

1 Write names on slips of paper and draw names.
2 Then spend one family devotion time discussing prayer requests. (Privacy can be protected by doing this interview-style as opposed to all together.)

3 Agree to pray for each other every day. Even young children can say 'Bless Andy and help him to do well at school'. So don't exclude any child old enough to understand the request.
4 Rotate partners every month.

You'll find far fewer arguments among children who pray for each other's needs. And children need to hear concerns expressed by parents, in order to see them as people.

Creative graces for meals

You needn't always pray the same prayers at mealtimes. Experiment with these or any others you can find.

Come, dear Lord Jesus, be our guest,
And bless what thou hast given us.

German grace

Praise God from whom all blessings
      flow
Praise Him all creatures here below,
Praise Him above ye heavenly host
    Praise Father, Son and Holy Ghost.

Doxology – sung or spoken

Scripture songs

Portions of Scripture set to music. Available in both songbooks and on tapes. Look out Ian Whyte's Psalms 1, 2 and 3 at a Christian bookshop.

Be present at our table, Lord,
Be here and everywhere adored,
Thy creatures bless and grant that we
May feast in paradise with thee.

> Amen
>
> John Wesley

We thank you for the world so sweet,
We thank you for the food we eat.
We thank you for the birds that sing.
We thank you God for everything.

> Amen

Bless, dear Lord, my daily food
Make me strong and make me good.

For every cup and plateful
God make us truly grateful.

Some ha'e meat, and canna eat,
And some wad eat that want it,
But we ha'e meat, and we can eat,
And sae the Lord be thankit.

> Robert Burns

Blessed art thou, O Lord our God,
King of the Universe, who bringest
forth bread from the earth.

> Jewish blessing

All good gifts around us,
Are sent from heaven above
Then thank the Lord, O thank the
  Lord, for all his love.

> German hymn by Matthias Claudius

Easy family Bible studies

The simpler the approach to Scripture, the better for children. Try reading a passage and then taking turns answering the following questions:

1 who was the central character?
2 what was the main point or main event?
3 where did the action take place?
4 when did it happen?
5 why is this information/event important to my life?
6 how does this passage relate to me, here and now?

By the time you've answered these six questions, you (and the children) will know the main points of the passage.

Finally, give the passage a title of three words or less to summarise the main theme.

Two little eyes to look to God;
Two little ears to hear his word;
Two little feet to walk in his ways;
Two little lips to sing his praise;
Two little hands to do his will
And one little heart to love him still.

Anonymous

Ideas for family Bible times

1 Write out a Bible verse, rebus style (i.e. draw symbols to replace the words).

2 Playact an interview with a biblical person. This works best when children interview parents. Then when the children know the story they can interview each other.

3 Have older children write a Bible story as a newspaper article. A project for energetic ones would be to put together a newspaper on the theme of the resurrection or Christmas or some other major biblical event.

4 Make cards with the names of the books of the Bible on them to memorise the order in which they are arranged.

5 Make your own 'Bible trivia' cards and play as a family.

6 Play Bible 'concentration' by making your cards with questions and answers or biblical names. Then place them all face down on the floor or table. One card is turned up and then another. If they match, the player gets to keep them. If not they are turned face down again and you try to remember where

they are when a match to one of them is turned up. The player with the most pairs, wins.

7 Suggest that children write a letter to God.

8 When weather permits, hold a sunset (or sunrise) meditation in your garden or a nearby park.

9 Act out any Bible scene for memory retention.

10 Write a Bible verse on a card. Then cut into jigsaw pieces and play as a puzzle to learn a verse.

11 Teaching children hymns is a great way of adding to their faith. The songs stick in your memeory and come back to mind when needed. (This is especially good if you have a piano at home and can sing together around it.)

Discipline equals discipleship?

Discipline has received a bad reputation and undeservedly so. Discipline is a necessity for all of us and we need to view it as a friend and not a punishment.

So, first take a look at your attitude to discipline in your own life. Do you shudder at the thoughts of getting up earlier, dieting or regular exercise – *because* you just don't want to discipline yourself? Most of us would admit to shying away from discipline. Yet, we see it as inevitably needful in regard to our children. We don't tell them they may brush their teeth when they like, or not eat brocccoli or sleep till noon on school days. We discipline them for their good. Discipline is a friend to their development as responsible individuals.

So how do we view discipline in regard to their less-than-perfect behaviour? We need a balanced, 'discipline is their friend' view here as well.

To make sure we discipline properly and without calling it punishment, consider the following biblical guidelines to disciplining children:

1 Discipline must be preceded by the parents 'practising what they preach'. Matthew 5:15 – 'Let your light shine . . .'
2 Children should be instructed in the right ways and know what is expected of them. Proverbs 22:6 – 'Train up a child in the way he should go . . .'
3 Never discipline in anger, taking out your frustration on the child. Rather, calmly explain to the child what wrong has been done and what the right behaviour in this situation would have been. Ephesians 4:26-27 – 'In your anger, do not sin . . .'
4 Put your arms around your child or set them on your lap while you explain to them why you must discipline them for this wrong. Ephesians 4:32 – 'Be kind and compassionate to one another . . .'
5 Make sure the punishment is appropriate to the crime and not over-reaction on your part. Proverbs 18:5 – 'It is not good to . . . deprive the innocent of justice.'

All this may sound like a lot of work but consider your goal. You want to set patterns of behaviour, and indeed, patterns of discipline, in their own lives – not just to punish the little beast for upsetting you!

Once you set this pattern of lovingly disciplining, you'll have far less need for discipline. They will see *why* you get upset about lying or fighting, and begin to think and act accordingly. You can change their view of discipline. But first, your own . . .

Five rules for happiness to teach your children

Emphasise these five rules and save your children a lot of grief in life.
1 The grass is NOT greener anywhere else. Life is what you make it. Help them avoid the 'if only . . .' syndrome at all costs.
2 Keep a close watch on attitudes. The Bible provides excellent guidelines for attitude checks in the Sermon on the Mount, Matthew 5, 6, 7.
3 Give yourself away to others if you really want to be happy. St Ignatius of Loyola says:

Fallen man loves to be his own master, to be independent, to act according to his own will. Here is the source of all his misery. He seeks himself and is unhappy. He indulges his passions and becomes their slave . . . On the other hand,, to serve God is to enjoy peace and freedom.

The Spiritual Exercises of
St Ignatius of Loyola

pub. Robert Scott, 1919

4 Appreciate, appreciate, appreciate – others around you, what you have. God and all creation. It's amazing how many blessings we have when we begin to count them.

5 Put yourself wholeheartedly into whatever needs doing.

Whatever you do, work at it with all your heart, as working for the Lord, not men, since you know that you will receive an inheritance from the Lord as a reward. It is the Lord Christ whom you are serving.

Colossians 3:23-25

These five attitudes can make your life. Try them and see.

Good books: friends for life

I wish I knew how many books I have read in my lifetime. I would guess that half to three-quarters of my education has come from reading. (I am not a telly watcher. I much prefer imagining the heroine's beauty to seeing her.)

We began reading to our girls by the time their eyes could focus. We are still reading to them. (We read a chapter each evening of the *Chronicles of Narnia* by C.S. Lewis.)

Elizabeth, at five, has just started reading and is absolutely thrilled with the miracle of making sense of the letters on the page. She would rather read than eat – just as I always did.

Why am I labouring the point? Because the books (or lack of them) in your house will surely shape your children's minds.

Fill your house with good books – Christian and classics of children's literature. They will do well in school and, ultimately, better in life.

1 Order Christian magazines for all age levels in your household.
2 Support Christian bookstores by buying Christian novels for your children to read. (They even stock teen romances with a Christian context. Check out what's available these days!)
3 Check around for Christian video companies and those that stock family movies.
4 Watch the example you are setting in what you read. Your children *do* notice.
5 Stay aware of what your children are reading. Censor certain books and TV programmes. Reading trash is wasting God's time.
6 Read together as a family. Not only is it a warm, satisfying activity, it sets the example before your children of the importance of reading good books.

By now you have decided that I am a book-aholic. Yes, I admit it. I also credit it with a great share of my success and enjoyment in life.

Shelter vs. exposure

Another suggestion (offered very carefully) for nurturing your children is to expose them to *all* types of people.

Obviously, this must be done with great care, but the more types of people you can introduce to your children, the better prepared they'll be to meet life on their own.

Sheltering your children from evil in the world will only make them more curious. They must meet the world directly someday; better to begin with Mum and Dad there to act as buffers.

1 Don't avoid driving through the worst areas of cities. Children need to see how all types of people live.
2 Make sure they see as many documentaries on other cultures as possible.
3 Visit other cultures whenever possible: investigate other races and different ways of living.
4 Censor their telly watching, but occasionally watch together a programme otherwise off-limits. Then discuss the values (or lack of them) portrayed. (e.g. 'What if Daddy was visiting another woman when he goes away on business?')
5 Discuss the types of people who sell drugs to children, etc., to alert your children to what the world is like for

those who oppose God's law of love.
6 Also, include in this education by exposure, people from different faiths or other nations – as a source of differentness.

Children need to learn that *different* does not equal *wrong*.

Exposure to life won't corrupt your children. Done in the context of family, it can help them to pray for a world lost without Jesus, and prepare them to help bring in the Kingdom of God.

Parents are . . .

Parents, what on earth are you supposed to be doing? Six things:

1 Acting as *God's representatives* (until the time your children can begin to know Him for themselves).
2 Acting as *providers* for their spiritual, physical and emotional needs.
3 Acting as their *trainers/instructors* in Christian values and common sense.
4 Living with them as their *friends*.
5 Acting as *correctors* when they go off the narrow path.
6 Living as *examples* before them of what God wants them to grow up to be.

All of this is nurture.

Books to help parents nurture children

Thorson's Series: *I need a Book*, **Tony Bradman**. (Parents' guides to special needs, such as going to the dentist, pets, disabilities, divorce, starting school.)

What is a Family?, **Edith Scheaffer**, Highland Books, 1983.

Hide or Seek, **James Dobson**, Hodder Christian Paperbacks, 1982.

Dr Dobson Answers Questions on Confident, Healthy Families, Kingsway Books, 1987.

Adolescence, **Anne Townsend**, Marshall Pickering, 1982. (For parents of adolescents.)

Families Matter, **Ed. Richard Whitfield**, Marshall Pickering. (Put out by the National Family Trust.)

Abuse Within the Family, **Anne Townsend**, Creative Publishing and Care Trust.

Raising Positive Kids in a Negative World, **Zig Ziglar**, Highland Books, 1986.

Children at Risk, **David Porter**, Kingsway Books, 1987.

Step Parenting, **Christine Atkinson**, Thorsons, 1986. (Kids' experiences of divorce.)

Bible story books

Lion Children's Bible, Lion Books, 1985.

Ladybird Bible Story Book, SU/Ladybird, 1983.

Lion Story Bible, Lion, a series of 52 individual Bible stories, 1984-88.

Fount Children's Bible, Fount, 1981.

The Children's Bible, Hamlyn. (My favourite for ten years – used and still using with both girls.)